Pagan Portals

Dream Analysis
Made Easy

Everything You Need to Know to Harness
the Power of Your Dreams

Pagan Portals

Dream Analysis Made Easy

Everything You Need to Know to Harness
the Power of Your Dreams

Krystina Sypniewski

**MOON
BOOKS**

Winchester, UK
Washington, USA

JOHN HUNT PUBLISHING

First published by Moon Books, 2023
Moon Books is an imprint of John Hunt Publishing Ltd., No. 3 East Street, Alresford
Hampshire SO24 9EE, UK
office@jhpbooks.net
www.johnhuntpublishing.com
www.moon-books.net

For distributor details and how to order please visit the 'Ordering' section on our website.

Text copyright: Krystina Sypniewski 2022

ISBN: 978 1 80341 178 1
978 1 80341 179 8 (ebook)
Library of Congress Control Number: 2022935545

A CIP catalogue record for this book is available from the British Library.

Design: Matthew Greenfield

UK: Printed and bound by CPI Group (UK) Ltd, Croydon, CR0 4YY
Printed in North America by CPI GPS partners

We operate a distinctive and ethical publishing philosophy in all areas of our business, from our global network of authors to production and worldwide distribution.

Contents

"Dreams transport us each and every night into that strange and radiant world inside ourselves wherein... we come face to face with powers greater than ourselves."
~ **James Hagan** author of *Diamonds of the Night: Search for the Spirit within Your Dreams*

Introduction

Navigating even day to day life can, at times, be a difficult and stressful work in progress. Then there are those unexpected things which, without any warning, crash into our lives and leave us reeling with shock. In confusion and in search of help, many of us turn to psychics, tarot readers, or other forms of divination in an effort to see what lies ahead, perhaps hoping for a change of circumstances, or believing that forewarned is forearmed. Some of us, despite demanding, busy schedules, try to carve out a few hours to focus on understanding ourselves and our connection to our universe. We may practice yoga or meditation. We may listen to talks by spiritual leaders or join discussion groups with like-minded others. We may enroll on courses designed to improve our knowledge of various shamanic or spiritual practices, or which claim to pass down ancestral guidance or cosmic wisdom from ascendant masters. Others might take part in 'spiritual tourism' and travel to sacred places in the hope that this will bring about some kind of opening up of our natural psychic abilities which will better help us to understand the purpose of our existence here, on our beautiful Mother Earth.

All of these methods of guidance have merit but there is one method which everyone has access to and which you can work with without ever having to travel. You don't need to set aside large chunks of time from your daily life, and the cost is negligible. So, what is it, and why, you may ask, isn't everyone using it? Well, what it is, is your dreams. If you learn to understand the language of your dreams, they will provide you with all the information you need as you walk life's path. Why isn't everyone already looking to their dreams for guidance? It's my thought that sometimes the very thing that is right in front of you, is the very thing you miss seeing. And I have to hold my hand up here. From a very early age, I experienced predictive dreams which were so clear and powerful that, all these years later, I still have no trouble recalling them. But it took a long while for me to realize just what an amazing guidance system dreams can be, if we take them seriously, and to turn my focus on learning their language.

There are, let's be honest, a ton of books out there about dreams and their interpretations. There are those comprising of lists of symbols which the reader is supposed to accept as pertaining to everyone universally. There are also those which offer some guidance on how to work out the meaning of dreams based on the author's interpretation of symbols and dreamscapes.

So why write another? Well, different people respond to different stimuli and have different ways of processing information. What works for one rarely, if ever, definitively works for all. Also, my belief is that each individual has their own associations and resonance with the contents of their dreams and that the information provided is specific to those associations and that resonance and can only be fully understood within that context.

In writing this book I'm using specific examples of the different types of dreams, along with a detailed look at how I decoded them, in order to provide a road map rather than one more overview.

Hopefully, the reader will find in these pages something which will ease the way for those just dipping their toe into the powerful and dynamic world of dream work, as well as a system for deepening the intuition and understanding of those already using the potent information contained within dreams to their advantage. More importantly, my wish is to empower the reader to be able to interpret their own dreams rather than having to seek out someone to do it for them.

Chapter 1

The Different Stages of Sleep

Dreaming is essential to our creativity and health. It is a fundamental part of being human. In the earliest part of the night, we close our eyes and fall into a deep sleep which lasts between 90 and 100 minutes and is known as Non-REM or non-synchronized sleep. Non-REM sleep has three different stages which link to specific brain waves and neuronal activity. During one of these phases, lasting around 10 to 20 minutes, the brain stem gives off pulses of electrical activity that gradually shift to the primary visual cortex, the area of the brain that controls the eyes. At this point the body develops a type of muscular immobility called atonia, caused by the total relaxation of the muscles. Although the body is now deeply relaxed, the mind is in a state of semi-wakefulness.

As REM (rapid eye movement) sleep takes over, the eyes begin to move beneath the lids. It is during this period that most of our dreaming takes place. Interestingly, although the pulses of electrical activity have shifted to the primary visual cortex, the REM phase is not a function of vision. Fetuses and people without sight are known to experience the same phenomenon.

When the REM phase is over, the dreamer enters another 90-100 minutes of Non-REM sleep, followed by another 10 or so minutes of REM. As the night advances, the amount of Non-REM, or deep sleep, within a cycle decreases, while the amount of REM or dreaming sleep correspondingly increases. This is why we experience our most vivid dreams towards morning. Most people sleep between six and eight hours per night. Which means, every night, whether you remember them or not, you experience four to six dreams.

The first dream of the night is usually quite short and is

generally, although perhaps cloaked in dream symbolism, a replay of an emotionally significant occurrence experienced by the dreamer during the day.

As the night progresses, our dreams get longer and move away from rehashing what has taken place and our consciousness, no longer tethered, ranges far and wide.

Chapter 2

Dreams and Their Many Uses

Throughout history many individuals have placed great store on their dreams and the information revealed in the silent hours of the night while our bodies rest and rejuvenate. The present day is no different, many people will insist that dreams can predict your future and that paying attention to their content can warn you of, and sometimes avert, difficulties.

In the words of Edgar Cayce, who was known as the sleeping prophet, *"Dreams are today's answers to tomorrow's questions."*[1]

For more than forty years, Edgar Cayce used the sleep state to provide help and information to those who searched him out. Given the name and location of a person anywhere in the world, he could provide answers to the questions posed on that person's behalf. He also possessed the ability to read other people's dreams so well, he could make the dreamer aware of potentially negative situations, spiritual or physical, and accordingly offer advice on how to overcome or avoid such. To him, the dream was an open book. He could tell from the information contained within it whether the person he was advising was the victim of an ill-wisher who was scheming behind their back, or if an illness they were presently unaware of was looming. He could also diagnose any illness the dreamer was suffering from and what was needed to bring them back to health. One of his cures involved a young woman who had been placed in a mental institution due to her unstable behavior. Cayce said her mental illness was caused by a bad tooth. Her family followed his advice and had the tooth removed and the girl recovered her sanity.

Far from being a quack, Cayce was years ahead of his time in emphasizing the importance of treating a person holistically, and the role that such things as diet, exercise and emotion play in a person's overall wellbeing. The diet he recommended all those years ago is what we now know as the Mediterranean diet.

In his sleep state, Cayce also made some notable predictions. Amongst them, four years before it happened, he prophesied World War II. He also foretold the finding of the Dead Sea Scrolls, as well as the discovery of the chamber under the Sphinx. One of his predictions most relevant to us today was that all manner of diseases would one day be diagnosed in a single drop of blood. Well, we're not quite there yet but I don't think anyone would deny that we are well on our way. Another of his foretellings very relevant to our modern-day world was that ocean levels would rise.

When asked where he derived his information from, he stated that in the sleep state the conscious mind becomes subjugated to the soul mind and can communicate with other minds, and with the universal soul force or akashic records.

As far as I'm aware, his organization is the only one remaining actively involved in the research of dreams in this way. Although, of course, there are many scientific studies, as well as shamanic practitioners who still place great value on dreams and their interpretations.

Edgar Cayce, though, was not the first to use dreams as an interpretive and healing tool. As far back as the ancient Sumerian civilization, cuneiform inscriptions record dreams experienced by Gudea, the ruler of the Mesopotamian city-state of Lagash. South American and Native American Indian tribes, amongst others, have traditionally highly regarded the power of dreams. Individuals, through prayer, fasting, and solitary, extended vigils, sought visions of their destiny from their dreams, seeking an image with which to create a personal link with the Spirit pervading all life. These dream visions connected the young man or woman to their life purpose within the group and facilitated the passage from youngster to adult. Details vary from tribe to tribe as to when and how such dreams were sought, but there is one constant: the visionary dream was held as sacred.

Sometimes the way of seeking these visions was a quiet and private affair, the seeker retiring to their lodge. Sometimes the method was drastic; young braves piercing their flesh with hooks and suspending themselves from poles.

Ancient Chinese tradition held that it is your soul which creates your dreams, leaving the body to its rest while it travels to other realms and meets other souls.

In Egypt, inside the shrine of Imhotep there are records of various dream interpretations. The Egyptian's believed in the power of dreams so strongly that they built dream or sleep temples. These temples were hospitals of sorts, healing a variety of ailments. The therapies involved chanting, placing the patient into a trance-like or hypnotic state, and analyzing their dreams in order to decide the course of treatment. The care plans included meditation, fasting, baths, and sacrifices to the patron deity or other spirits

Sleep temples also existed in the Middle East and istikhara, a special prayer recited just prior to sleep, was used to summon dream guidance. Ancient Greece also boasted sleep temples and both Hippocrates, regarded as the father of medicine, and Aristotle, Greek philosopher and scientist, who is still considered one of the greatest thinkers in politics, psychology and ethics, strongly advocated the power of dreams in the treatment of illnesses. The Greek treatment was referred to as incubation and focused on prayers to Asclepios, the Greek god of healing.

A similar Hebrew method known as Kavanah involved focusing on letters of the Hebrew alphabet which spelled out the name of God.

For many people, the ultimate authority on all matters is the Bible, in which instances of prophetic dreams abound. Joseph isn't just renowned for his splendid, many-colored coat. He was also a prophetic dreamer and could analyze the dreams of others. Called before Pharaoh, he correctly interpreted Pharaoh's dream of seven fat cows on the banks of the Nile being devoured by seven lean cows, as well as his dream of seven healthy ears of grain being devoured by seven meagre ears of grain. Pharaoh had first summoned all of the wise men and magicians in Egypt, but no one was able to tell him the meaning of the dreams.

When Joseph correctly interpreted them to mean that seven years of plentiful harvests would be followed by seven years of famine, the Pharaoh wisely believed him and followed Joseph's counselling that the only way to prevent disaster was to store surplus grain during the years of plenty with which to feed the people during the years of want. Joseph travelled all over Egypt, building granaries and ordering farmers to store one fifth of their harvests.

Following seven years of plenty, famine did indeed strike and people came from far and wide to buy food from Egypt, thus bringing it wealth and status as a powerful Mediterranean nation.[2]

Both of the Pharaoh's dreams contain the same message and although the symbolism is quite simple, the dreams are of major import, as highlighted by the repetition of their message. It isn't quite the power of three, but we know that when the information in a prophetic dream is repeated in this way, the message is of particular significance. The Qur'an also makes mention of dreams, including those had by the prophet Muhammad.

There is clear evidence that the information provided by dreams was held in high regard in powerful ancient civilizations, but there are also more contemporary indications that your dreams can provide answers to help you solve any manner of problem. Indeed, some of our greatest inventions arose out of dreams. The idea for the sewing machine came to its inventor Elias Howe in a dream in 1845. Dreaming he was about to be cooked by cannibals, he noticed their spears as they waved them in an up and down motion while dancing around a fire. He saw that at the tip of each spear was a small hole. Awaking, he realized that having the hole in the needle close to the point, instead of at the traditional end, could be key to a sewing machine that worked.

Einstein's theory of relativity came about out of a childhood dream in which he was sledding. As the sled gathered speed, it seemed to the young boy to approach the very speed of light. The stars distorted, transforming into colors and patterns. In fact, Einstein felt his entire career could be viewed as an extension of that profound dream.

James Watson, who, together with Francis Crick, discovered the double helix structure of DNA is said to have dreamed of a spiral staircase, giving him the idea of how DNA might be constructed.

Chemist Dimitry Mendeleev spent ten years trying to create a pattern that connected the chemical elements together. One night, he fell asleep and dreamed the answer to his puzzle, giving birth to the periodic table. Writing in his diary, Mendeleev said, *"I saw in a dream a table where all the elements fell into place as required. Awakening, I immediately wrote it down on a piece of paper."*[3]

Frederick Grant Banting and his colleague, John James Rickard Macleod were awarded the Nobel-Prize for the discovery of insulin. The idea for the experiment which led to this major life-saving invention came to Banting in a dream he had one night.

These examples are only a few. There are many, many, more. There are also countless ideas for films, songs, and books whose creators attribute their inspiration to dreams, including Samuel Taylor Coleridge's epic poem Kubla Khan and Jung's *The Red Book,* as well as Stephen King's *Dreamcatcher.* The Beatles song, *Yesterday,* came to Paul McCartney in a dream. After which he spent months asking people if they had heard the tune before, thinking he must have unconsciously plagiarized it. There are even people who have won the lottery and insist the numbers came to them in a dream.

Obviously, then, prophetic dreams can yield big dividends!

Despite that, there are those who insist that dreams are simply the brain re-hashing life events. And, of course, some are. Does that, then, mean we should dismiss them as purposeless? Or does their benefit lie in the fact that they provide the dreamer with the opportunity to review what took place from a different angle and perhaps gain valuable insights into colleagues, friends, partners, jobs, themselves – the list is endless – allowing them to modify behavior or make beneficial life changes. Sometimes our dreams are epic, but they don't all have to be in order to be helpful.

This is a dream a friend told me about:

Last week I ordered some ear drops for Ginger (a cat) and then forgot about it as they said the earliest they could deliver would be Monday or perhaps Tuesday this week. Then last night (Tuesday), out of the blue, I had a dream that I received a message saying the drops would be delivered late.

I woke up and thought, what day is it? It was Wednesday. And I knew to watch out for the drops being delivered. While I was eating breakfast, an email arrived to tell me they would be delivered by 9 p.m., confirming my dream. So, I might have forgotten about them, but my brain obviously hadn't.

This is not a high-octane dream. Whilst mildly prophetic – it predicts the delivery of the drops – the content is pretty average stuff. But was it useful? Well, it alerted my friend to the fact the drops would be delivered, enabling him to organize his day to make sure he was in when they came, thus avoiding the delay and work involved in arranging for them to be either collected or redelivered. Life changing? No. But decidedly helpful.

You might, correctly, point out that the email did the same thing. But it's possible the email might have gone unnoticed, perhaps landing in the 'junk' file, or because my friend, with a busy day ahead, hadn't checked his emails before leaving the house. It's also possible that the brain and the superconscious just don't take modern technology into account. Whatever alternatives present themselves, none of them take away from the fact that my friend's dream had value.

How about this one?

I dreamed I was in town. It was dark and my little black cat, Mu-mu was with me. I was afraid we might get separated and that she would get lost and not know how to get home again, or that she might get run-over, or someone might get hold of her and harm her.

I was frantic, trying to catch her. Suddenly, a voice said, 'She's all right. Everything is all right. Let her go.' All my fear washed away, and I relaxed.

How many of you have already labelled this as an anxiety dream? Just the mind churning over day-to-day worries and using the symbol of a pet cat to personify them.

Would it surprise you then, to know that a few weeks later this dreamer's cat suffered kidney failure and had to be euthanized? The dreamer was devastated by the loss of her furry family member but took great comfort from her dream, knowing that, as the voice had promised, her beloved cat, wherever she was, was going to be all right.

There is also an important category of dreams known as lucid dreaming. With this type of dream, the person is aware they are dreaming. So what, you might ask? What's the big woo-ha about recognizing you're in a dream? Knowing you are dreaming opens up a whole raft of possibilities, from simply having fun, to the seriously life changing. After all, if you are aware of being in a dream, might you be able to take charge of what is happening? And if you can alter the outcome of a dream, can you, then, also alter the pertaining situation in real life?

I have long held the belief that while we can hold sway over some aspects of our future, there are other, bigger, issues which it is our destiny to meet and through which we learn to know ourselves. But this does not, in any way, invalidate the idea that lucid dream work can influence the outcome of major life events in a positive way.

Truly, even those dreams which are simple wish fulfillment can serve a purpose in alerting the dreamer to unmet goals and desires and their true-life purpose.

Chapter 3

The Basics

By now, hopefully, you can see that far from being a new idea, the roots of the belief in the importance of dreams are old and grow from, and are grounded in, fertile soil. Not only that, dreams, and their meanings, also have prominence in the science of psychology. As Carl Jung says:

> The dream is often occupied with apparently very silly details, thus producing an impression of absurdity, or else it is on the surface so unintelligible as to leave us thoroughly bewildered.
> Hence, we always have to overcome a certain resistance before we can seriously set about disentangling the intricate web through patient work.
> But when at last we penetrate to its real meaning, we find ourselves deep in the dreamer's secrets and discover with astonishment that an apparently quite senseless dream is in the highest degree significant, and that in reality it speaks only of important and serious matters.
> This discovery compels rather more respect for the so-called superstition that dreams have a meaning.[4]

There are those rare individuals, like Casey, for whom understanding the meanings of dream symbolism comes as easily as breathing. For most of us, though, it requires some research, particularly when starting out. As with anything, the more you put into working with your dreams, the more you will get out of them.

Each night the average person spends approximately ninety minutes in a REM dream state. Some dreamers can remember all or the majority of everything they dream, others have trouble remembering even the smallest fragment of the occasional dream. A few individuals will say they don't dream. The truth is, the more attention you pay to your dreams, the more you will begin to remember. So, the first priority is to treat your dreams seriously and give thanks for the guidance you receive through them. If you neglect to honor the counsel given to you in this way, then you can't really expect too much in terms of a deep connection. Although not necessary, it is helpful prior to sleep to set an intention to remember your dreams. Say a little prayer, use an affirmation or simply focus on the fact that you will dream tonight. Whatever you are comfortable with will work best for you.

Of course, before any effective work with your dreams is possible, you need to be able to recall the content. If you sleep alone, then the quickest and easiest way is to speak your dream into a recorder of some type which you keep to hand beside the bed. If this isn't possible then a notepad and pen or pencil (and perhaps a flashlight) is the next best thing. If you awaken out of a dream, this recording of the content is best done straight away. Otherwise, do this first thing in the morning, before getting out of bed. Some people will see a quick and dramatic improvement in recall, but for most it will take a bit of time and consistent practice before they see appreciable results.

You also need to keep a dream diary. I can hear you groaning already! Why always the insistence on keeping a dream diary? Well, the thing is – hindsight is a wonderful attribute. Keeping a dream diary will help you to look back and identify the pattern and verify the meaning of your dreams, as well as aiding you in classifying what category they belong to. Also, when we write something down, for some inexplicable reason, it tends to stay in our consciousness longer and a small part of our brain turns it over at a subconscious level, therefore focusing energetically, be it only low key, on the subject matter. Over time, this becomes habitual and aids us in both remembering and interpreting our dreams.

Your dream diary can be as simple or complicated an affair as you would wish. I've never used an actual diary as when I first started to write down my dreams there could be days or even weeks when I didn't recall anything, so having set pages meant I would have wasted a lot of paper. Instead, I chose a nice, A4, lined, book with an interesting cover and pages made from real tobacco leaves. I've kept to this format as, even though I now recall a much higher percentage of my dreams, doing this means I can arrange the content to my own, personal, tastes. I also enjoy being able to take out my dream diary and savor a pretty, different, or in some way interesting cover. I've even personalized covers, using stick on butterflies and rainbows or sparkly stars and moons and angels.

I separate the pages into sections, with short headings of the subject matter my dreams are likely to contain: Mum and Dad; Animals; Help; Nightmares; Dead People; Buildings; Nature, and so on, which enables me to group my dreams together and saves me from wading through numerous pages if I want to refer back to a particular dream. I list the date of the dream and I write any colors it may have featured (colors are important and easily forgotten) at the end of the description. I note how the dream felt and anything that may have been said or any other sounds I may have heard. I also write down any symbols or words which stood out to me. This way, if I notice something has happened which I can relate to a dream I didn't understand at the time, or if something unexpected or unusual happens around the time I had the dream, I can easily go back and make a note and reconsider the content to see if the meaning is now clearer. It's also an easy and effective way to keep track of predictive dreams. This is particularly helpful to those just starting out on dream interpretation. A dream diary is very useful, too, for repetitive dreams which you can't immediately make sense of. Of course, not all dreams will fit into an already existing section. In this case, it is easy to let the dream begin a new section.

You might also wish to construct a dream dictionary. You might want to use a separate book for this as you may complete a diary long before you complete your dictionary, although, initially, using the end pages of your diary may suffice as you can then update the dictionary each time you start a new diary.

Whichever way you choose, the idea of a dictionary is that as you begin to ascribe definite, and personal to you, meanings to symbols, you can make a note of these to refer to when they reappear in your dreams.

Occasionally, over time, the meaning of a symbol may change. You may, for example, have grown up viewing religion as oppressive and representative of a lack of control over your life, or dismissed it as invalid, and therefore religious icons may have held a negative connotation for you, but having in adulthood discovered a religion, spiritual path or deity in accordance with your values, it may be that you now hold a different, positive, view.

Chapter 4

Dream Symbols

Although it is essential you interpret your dreams in a personal way, there are a few symbols which are pretty much accepted as having a universal meaning.

The House

The house represents the dreamer. If the house is a specific dwelling with which the dreamer has a very strong and unique past association, then the house represents either the fear of, or possible recurrence of the situation the dreamer associates with that house.

The Car

Again, this represents the dreamer, or perhaps more specifically, the direction that the dreamer is taking. Even if the dreamer has particular associations with a car, whether happy or sad or even terrifying, the car still represents the dreamer's journey through life. The trick here is to add the association to the symbol. So: The car + happy feelings or memories = the dreamer is happy or will shortly be so. The car + an association of something terrifying = the dreamer is in a bad situation or may be about to find themselves so or, at the very least, is worried that they may.

There is, of course, also the possibility that a dream about your car which informs of an accident or a break-down is telling you just that: watch out for accidents when driving – or your car may be about to break-down. In the case of a dream featuring either of the above scenarios, the context of your life will point you toward the right conclusions. If your work and private relationships are sound and in a good state, then you may need to look toward the practical.

Water

While not quite as definitive as the other two symbols, water is so often associated with the emotions that if it enters your dream, you should examine this aspect first.

Butterfly

The butterfly is pretty much universally thought to symbolize transformation because of its own distinct change from caterpillar to butterfly. In his fascinating and persuasive book, *Proof of Heaven*, Eben Alexander describes how, during his near-death experience, he had no awareness of his body and how instead his awareness rode on a butterfly's wing.

What is often neglected, though, is the struggle the pupa goes through to emerge in beauty.

Death

Dreaming of death or dying, your own or someone else's, rarely portends the actual death of someone. It almost always, like the number nine, signifies closure: something coming to an end.

Standard Symbols

If you have a book of dream symbols, particularly when just beginning this work, it can kick-start your subconscious into providing relevant meanings. If a dream book interpretation resonates, great! Job done. If not, do the detective work.

I have a very old dream book which, when I initially started taking my dreams seriously and began working with them, I used a lot. One of its interpretations is that dreaming of feces is a sign you will come into money. Well, that never did resonate with me, and, after several such dreams, I realized that, for me, dreaming of feces meant I was about to be dumped on.

The most important thing to remember, always, when working with your dreams is to first apply your own associations to any symbol. A church, to one person, may hold nothing but happy, positive memories. For another, a church may symbolize repression and unhappiness. Likewise, someone might dream of a magpie, and, if they know the rhyme, may immediately regard it as an omen of sorrow. Whereas someone I know, who is unfamiliar with the rhyme, sees magpies as happy, bouncy, and attractive to the eye. If he were to dream of a magpie, his connotations would be entirely different, and he might well see it as a good omen.

Several nights ago, I dreamed of a black, mother cat. She had brought her two, black, kittens to show off to me. They were wearing red collars. Recounting this to a friend, she immediately said, 'Oh, that's not a good dream. Black cats are bad luck! And red is danger!'

Well, for me, all cats, and particularly black ones, symbolize good luck. And yes, red can signal danger but there is nothing else in the dream content which, to me, tells of misfortune and red is also associated with the life-force, fire, and passion. So, for me, this is a good dream, foretelling good luck and positive energy.

To further underscore the positive meaning in this dream, it was immediately followed by another of myself pushing a cart that served as a buggy, with a smiling, sublimely healthy and happy baby in it. The 'buggy' was low to the ground and the baby's head, although her wide-eyed gaze was fixed on the sky, almost touched the path. For me, this indicates that something new is coming into my life which will increase my creativity. The sky is a symbol of creative potential, and the ground indicates the material world. The two together are potential brought into manifestation. The baby is a symbol of new beginnings. Again, I would stress that these meanings are personal. Those same symbols could mean something completely different to someone else.

Giving the highest priority to your own associations also holds true for what I've termed universal symbols, although it is far less likely that those few signs will hold different meanings for individuals.

Feelings and Smell

Any feelings experienced during a dream provide vital clues and should be taken careful account of. Less common but equally important is any smell you may become aware of while dreaming.

Taste

Personally, I rarely taste anything in a dream, but I have worked with people who do. Obviously, just as with the sense of smell, any sense of taste holds vital information for the dreamer and should be taken note of.

Colors

Some people say they always dream in color, but I think for the majority dreams are usually staged in black and white. Dreaming in color, though, has great significance, and again the primary thing to look at is what associations the color holds for the dreamer. Also, for myself, if I dream in color, I know the dream comes from my higher self, is particularly relevant, and it's important to pay attention to it.

Here is a short list of colors and their meanings. Also, the chakras (energy centers) they align with, as often using both references adds depth to your understanding:

Red: Corresponds to the root chakra and is symbolic of Life force, anger, passion and sexuality, physical strength, action, the Holy Spirit, and also blood, martyrdom, danger and STOP.

Orange: Corresponds to the sacral chakra and symbolizes health, energy, and sensuality.

Yellow: Corresponds to the solar plexus chakra and its associations are willpower, humor, optimism, warmth, compassion, and intellect, but also cowardice. (N.B. Grey also symbolizes the mind and therefore the intellect.)

Green: Correspondences are the heart chakra, love, openness, acceptance of self and others, the highest healing and growth, but also jealousy. (N.B. For many people pink symbolizes love.)

Blue: Corresponds to the throat chakra and (as you would expect) communication, truth, integrity, and also hope.

Indigo: Corresponds to the third eye chakra and intuition, insight, imagination and the sixth sense.

Violet: Corresponds to the crown chakra and the higher-self, spiritual power, connectedness to all beings, mysticism, and magic.

White: Always stands for purity and innocence and a connection to All That Is.

Black: This is a color that absorbs all others. If it appears in a dream, it may be telling the dreamer that there is something they need to absorb. This could apply to many things; the dreamer might need to absorb a certain food or vitamin or be constitutionally lacking in some other way. However, it may be referring to information or a situation the dreamer is trying to ignore. It can, in some cases, when a person is withdrawn, be referring to life itself. It also stands for death, mourning, eternity, depression (grey can also signify depression) ignorance or fear.

Past, Present and Future

Usually, life circumstances will help to define which dream symbol represents the present. But if not immediately clear, then the past and future can be defined in several ways. My go to symbol is the left or right-hand side of the dreamscape, or it might be the path or road I'm traveling. Left, for me, represents the past and the right represents the future. Other things to look for which define the past are ancient buildings, old clothes, old things, especially if they were physically present in your past, even old people. Childhood scenes are linked to the past, as are dates in history. Another indication of past or future are moving objects. Objects coming toward you signify the future. While those receding or traveling away from you denote the past. As always, what resonates with the dreamer is the most powerful indicator of meaning.

A focus on, or the prominence of, the right side of something in a dream can also represent the realm of consciousness, which the dreamer might interpret as the dream referring to their conscious reality or something they are already aware of. Equally, a similar focus, or prominence, on the left side can represent the dreamer's unconscious or that which they are currently unaware of or are denying.

Dialogue

It probably goes without stating that anything spoken in the dream needs careful examination and attention. Sometimes a voice is heard even when the dreamer is alone in their dreamscape. Dr. Jung held this to be a most meaningful occurrence and identified the appearance of a voice in dreams as an intervention from the Self.

Numbers

It was the Pythagoreans in the 6th century BC who were one of the first groups to popularize the idea that numbers are not merely mathematical symbols, and that they actually carry spiritual significance. As Pythagoras was once quoted to have said, *"Number is the ruler of forms and ideas and the cause of gods and daemons."*[5]

Of all the dream symbols, when I was first starting out, numbers were the most impenetrable for me. Partly this was because there are, as any numerologist will tell you, definitive associations for each number, which doesn't seem to allow for any individual interpretation, although these vary widely depending on which source you use. I struggled with this for a while before I arrived at the obvious: numbers in dreams are no different to any other material. If someone has a particular association with a number, then that is significant and must be taken into consideration. One method that can be used is to combine any personal association for the individual with the numerological meaning to arrive at the message of the dream.

There are numerous books giving information regarding numerology, as well as articles and online blogs. Below is a list of the meanings which resonate for me:

Zero: For me, this number represents the primordial void and the realm of potential; that which precedes life; the eternal force. When this number appears in my dreams it tells me I stand on the threshold where anything is possible. I know that to move forward I will need to make a choice, a decision.

One: The number one is the basis for all numbers: one power, one spirit, one energy; known as the Universal Force, Creative Energy, or God. When this number appears, I know that a seismic shift is on its way, either within myself or in my circumstances. Either way, the shift is outside my control I will need to be focused, single minded and strong to ride the wave and to make the most of opportunity. This number often signals new beginnings.

Two: Two is a combination of one and one, but it also begins a division of the Whole, or the One. Therefore, the number two may make for strength, but it may also make for weakness.

The way I interpret this, when this number enters my dreams, is that it refers to something outside myself, usually another person, although not always (it could be work or some other situation), either already in my life, or perhaps about to come into my life. When I think of two in this way, then the idea of it signifying either strength or weakness makes perfect sense, as any significant person, whether friend or partner or family can either aid me on my journey through life, thereby strengthening me, or the relationship may prove to be detrimental and weakening to me. Similarly with work. A project may prove rewarding, or it could be something which will take my energy and time and provide little in return.

Usually, in my own experience, a dream involving this number will contain at the very least some sketchy information about the person the number is relevant to, even if it only indicates whether male or female or perhaps what role their relationship plays – are they friend or colleague or even, perhaps, a potential partner. Similarly, with an arising situation, there will at least be a hint of the direction this will come from.

If there is no additional information at all, then this dream will cause me to take stock of the people and situations around me to see how those relationships feel, and to consider carefully anything new which appears on my horizon.

Three: This is a powerful number. Three represents the divine principle that underlies life, as illustrated in the Godhead: The Father, The Son and The Holy Ghost, as well as many other triunes such as birth, life and death.

The number three features strongly in almost all spiritual traditions. There are three limbs to the Tree of Life. In Wicca we have the Maiden, Mother, and Crone. In Hinduism there are Brahma, Vishnu, and Shiva and indeed, all ancient beliefs are centered in the Trinity. Three, therefore, is a positive number, symbolic of success, intuition, and good fortune.

Four: The number four symbolizes the elements of earth, air, fire, and water. Also, the four corners of the earth and the four lower centers or natures of man. Therefore, four also symbolizes the body. When this number features in my dream, I know I need to pay attention to the here and now as it often appears when I'm over extended and feeling, in some way, vulnerable or insecure. It tells me I need to ground and stabilize myself. It can also be a warning to utilize self-discipline.

Five: For me, five has always been slightly ambiguous. At its best, it is a number signaling adventure, something different. It also relates to the five senses, so it's about what we feel and experience and often signals something enjoyable on its way. But it does have a more serious side and connects to weighty and not always happy life changes such as marriage, divorce, moving, or a new job or responsibility. So it can be a warning that important choices are imminent.

Six: The number six symbolizes beauty and the symmetrical forces. Six represents a balance between the earthly and spiritual realms and is aligned with intuition, clairvoyance, and other extrasensory capabilities, hence we talk about the sixth sense. When this number appears in my dream, I know that in order to really understand its significance to me at this time, I need to look hard at what else is going on in my dreamscape and also what is happening in my life.

Seven: The number seven is linked to the spiritual nature of man. The world was created in seven days or stages. There are seven days in the week. We have seven, main, chakras in our bodies and seven holes in our heads. There are seven candles on the Menorah, seven amens in the Gregorian chant. There were seven knots on Mohammed's golden rope, which hung from heaven, and mankind is said to possess seven virtues and seven deadly sins. Snow White (Divine within) had seven dwarfs and Jesus lifted the consciousness of Mary Magdalene by cleansing her of seven devils.

According to Cayce, seven symbolizes the spiritual forces. Seven, then, is a powerful and mystical number associated with truth seeking, spiritual growth and the search and attainment of wisdom.

Eight: The number eight, however, is a bit more complicated to explain. For me, this number has associations with time. Turned on its side, it is the symbol of infinity, and I also associate it with the idea that time is not linear and that everything, past, present and future, may in fact be happening all at once. To clarify, then, for me, eight is a flexible symbol, which I define according to the other contents of my dreamscape, rather than a fixed symbol. When it occurs in my dream, I also think in terms of balance – the conscious with the unconscious, the earthly with the spiritual. Depending on the other content of my dreamscape, I might examine the balance in my life – am I aligned with my life purpose? Am I neglecting my spiritual growth? Infinity is a long time to spend in regret. Better to be still a while and take stock.

Nine: The number nine is a mystical number connecting with higher purpose and the mission an individual has taken on in this lifetime. The number of fulfillment, and, according to traditional symbolism, representing the perfect form of the perfected Trinity in its threefold elevation. When this number shows up in my dream, it is a sign of imminent change in my life as nine signifies completion and endings to me.

It's perhaps worth mentioning that many numerologists

work only with the first nine numbers, adding higher figures together until they are reduced to single digits. This has quite possibly influenced my associations with the number nine, but, however I arrived at my understanding of the number, the association I have with it is valid and stands. In card reading, the nine of spades symbolizes death as the spade looks like a dead leaf.

Ten: The number ten also heralds completion but whereas nine can symbolize change and the end of a circumstance or event in our lives, ten represents the end of a cycle, usually associated with spiritual growth, perhaps, rarely, even attainment of enlightenment. It reflects the unity that is possible. A completion through a return to the ONE and a completely new life or beginning.

Eleven: For me, eleven is another ambiguous number. It is linked to destiny, and it can mean – pay attention! You are about to miss an important message from the Universe! Or it can mean – relax, you've got this! You're on track. So, another number where it is important to take into consideration the rest of the dreamscape and your life situation in interpreting its significance.

Twelve: Twelve is the number of cosmic order. It takes ritualistic form as the twelve apostles, the twelve signs of the Zodiac, the twelve months of the year, the twelve loaves of hallowed bread in the tabernacle of the Israelites, the twelve tribes of Israel, to mention only a few.

It is said that Jesus was born at midnight. The hour representing not only His completion and perfection, but also the necessity for that spiritual force to move into the earth to overcome worldly influences.

Therefore, a dream of the number twelve could represent

a powerful creative force about to enter your life or, if you are a creative, that your endeavor is being supported at the highest soul level.

These are meanings that resonate with me but there are lots of online and other resources which will offer different meanings. Whichever source resonates with you, and you decide to use as the basis for your own interpretation, that is the meaning which is correct for you.

Animals

Within this text, there are dreams which feature animals and I will have ascribed meanings to them in the context of the analysis. To be honest, if you look online, there are lots of sites offering completely different meanings for whatever animal you might want to look up. And there is a good reason for this as people have very strong personal associations with any particular animal which will vary according to experience and even culture and environment. For that reason, I'm only going to list the more common animals and those with which I have a strong association. And, at the risk of sounding like an automated message: The meaning YOU ascribe to a specific animal is the one that counts. Only consider other meanings if you're at a complete loss.

Ant: This humble creature is industrious and a terrific team worker. You have work to do.

Badger: Watch out! Someone is baiting you.

Bat: An important message is on its way. Something hidden will be revealed.

Bear: Strength and healing. Can also represent Mother Earth.

Beaver: Security and prosperity. Your hard work is paying off.

Bed bug: A small annoyance.

Bee: The bee is also industrious and another team worker. It is unselfish and works for the common good and brings sweetness into our lives.

Beetles: To me, they represent eternal life and rebirth.

Birds: A positive omen. You will be freed from your worries. Dreaming of songbirds may herald good news.

Birds' eggs: Money is coming to you. Or look to your savings (nest egg).

Butterfly: This beautiful creature signifies transformation of some sort, whether on the physical plane or on the inner planes.

Camel: The ship of the desert. You will leave your problems behind.

Canary: Gossip or someone revealing a secret.

Cat: Intuition and your psychic self. An appearance of one of the big cats in your dream can herald a test you will need to face.

Caterpillar: Hidden potential.

Cock: Someone acting from their ego.

Coyote: The coyote is traditionally seen as sly and a trickster. But for me this animal also possesses the qualities of perseverance and endurance.

Dog: Signifies loyalty and faithfulness, friendship, and protection.

Dolphin: Represents the freedom that comes with spiritual enlightenment. Wisdom.

Donkey: Stubbornness.

Dove: A symbol of peace; a person or a situation may be in need of this.

Dragon: A very powerful symbol of wisdom and the life force.

Eagle: The spiritual self and the gift of far-reaching clarity.

Elephant: Have you forgotten something important? Or is there a situation where you need to forgive and forget?

Fish: This can be a spiritual symbol. It also signifies wisdom or something 'fishy' going on.

Fox: The traditional interpretation here is of slyness or manipulation but for me the fox symbolizes a need to reconnect with the beauty of nature and the need for adaptability. It can also connect to physical attraction.

Frog: Beauty within.

Hare: A warning to look before you leap. Can also be

connected to the tides of the Moon and their influence upon matters of the Earth plane.

Hedgehog: A prickly situation needs handling with care.

Horse: You need to find the strength to act or make a choice quickly. The negative connotation is that someone is taking you for a ride.

Ladybird: A very positive symbol. Expect good luck or to hear good news.

Monkey: For many, the monkey is synonymous with Hanuman, and is seen as a trickster. But for me this animal also signifies socialness and fun. It can also signify aggression.

Mouse: Feeling insignificant or fearful.

Octopus: A period of solitude is on its way during which you will gain much wisdom.

Ostrich: There is something you don't want to face up to.

Otter: A fun and happy period is here, or on the horizon.

Owl: The owl is a motif for clear thinking and wisdom.

Peacock: Don't allow pride to prevent you asking for help.

Pegasus: Soul growth and inspiration.

Rabbit: Timidity.

Rat: You are allowing someone or a situation to gnaw at you.

Raven: A mystical creature, dreaming of a raven often means a message from the guides of the inner planes.

Robin: A positive symbol. When I dream of a robin it generally heralds communication I've been waiting on, and good news.

Snake: Spiritual awakening or growth. Wisdom. Temptation. Negative connotation, someone is not to be trusted.

Spider: The positive meaning would be that you are about to be busy. The negative is beware of walking into a trap or of being manipulated.

Stork: This is, of course, a well-known symbol of new beginnings or heralding a new addition to the family.

Swan: This is an aspect of the White Goddess. Also signifies beauty and grace. A black swan signifies the mystical realms and intuition.

Unicorn: The mystical and magical, spiritual growth and purity.

Vulture: There is a mess to clean up. Or needing to let go of something which is finished.

Wasp: Beware of someone bad mouthing you. Conversely, watch what you say about someone or some situation.

Whale: Deep wisdom, mysteries of the depths, Great Mara, and intuition.

Wolf: The wildness within, fortitude and a willingness to take your place within the pattern.

Worm: Earth mysteries and connection to nature mysteries. Preparatory work prior to something coming into being. Negative symbolism would be someone who is weak and perhaps not to be trusted.

Chapter 5

Dream Wisdom

My earliest recollection of a prophetic dream was one I had at the age of eight, when I dreamed that I was being operated on. I saw the surgeon take something out of my stomach, and because my knowledge of anatomy was zero at the time, on waking, I mentally decided it must be a baby, as that was the only thing I knew of that came out of a woman's stomach. In the dream, my hospital bed stood on a windowsill.

Almost seven months later, I developed acute appendicitis and was rushed into hospital for emergency surgery. During my stay, my bed was on a narrow annex to the main ward. The walls and roof of the annex were made entirely of glass – again, this type of annex wasn't something within my sphere of understanding at the time, hence the windowsill.

Which brings me to an important point. Our dreams will struggle to provide us with symbolism we can relate to, at least in some way. Just as my dream used a windowsill to describe something I would otherwise have been at a loss to understand, it is quite likely that, at least as a complete beginner, what Jung called the collective unconscious, and which I think of in terms of the collective superconscious, will try its level best to open a doorway you can recognize to enable you to step through into your dream world. I'm afraid, though, that there does seem to be an expectation of commitment to growth and, in my experience, the more you work with your dreams, the more complex the symbolism can be. Many of my own dream symbols now can't be found within any dream book.

You may be forgiven for thinking that my early experience should have been enough to convince me of the value of dreams and the information they contain, and that, therefore, my feet should have been firmly planted on the path of dream work from an early age. What can I say? I'm a slow learner. But I'm not alone in failing, initially, to place a high enough regard on what my dreams were telling me. The renowned Edgar Cayce, who helped so many, and a devout Christian, was at times fearful of his capabilities, believing they may have been given to him by the devil, and failed to use his skills when his son, Milton Porter, became ill. When Cayce finally used the sleep state to do a reading for Milton, it was too late, and the baby died. A harsher lesson I can't imagine.

As for myself, after that amazing dream at the age of eight, I remember very little of my dreams, there were certainly none I made any effort to record or analyze, until many, many years later when, while at university, doing an English/Imaginative Writing Degree, the tutor asked us to keep a dream diary and use it as a basis for short stories. As soon as I began to take account of them, my dreams intensified and became easier to recall. Unfortunately, it took a good few more years before I learned to honor the guidance they contained.

A good friend of mine would certainly have been better prepared if she had taken note of a series of dreams she had. This was her first dream as she recounted it to me.

The First Dream

In the dream it's raining. We're in the car. My husband's driving. The rain's hammering down and the wind's shrieking all around us and I'm scared because he's driving too fast. I tell him to slow down, but he won't.

I plead with him, but he takes no notice, so I open the door and leap out into the road. The next minute he loses control and plunges off the pier, into the sea. I start screaming and yelling for help but by the time they get to him, he's dead.

In my dream I think, that's the end of it – he's gone. But then, everywhere I go, I see him. He's turned into a zombie.

He starts chasing me through an empty department store. Everything's covered in dust sheets. And he keeps coming. Relentlessly! Coming.

And I'm running. Running higher and higher into the building. Finally, I'm on the roof. Trapped! And he's coming.

The next thing I remember is being back on the dark, rain-washed, deserted street. I get into my car and lock the door. I put on the seatbelt and I'm just about to start up the engine when, I glance at the passenger seat and ... he's there. He's staring at me, and I realize, I'm never going to escape from him. He'll never let me go.

She had this dream at the end of 1998. At the beginning of 1999 she had another dream.

The Second Dream

I'm driving along a road, following my husband in his car. After a short while the road split into two parallel lanes, the left running lower; the right running just above it. I take the higher road; my husband opts for the lower one. The dream continues with me walking and looking for our home but unable to find it. Eventually, I do. The lights are on, and when I knock at the door, a woman opens it.

Toward the middle of 1999 she had the final dream in this series.

The Third Dream

I'm walking through an apocalyptic landscape. All around me is devastation. I know everyone has caught a virus which has made them insane, and they have slaughtered each other. I come to a house and sat on the porch is a little puppy. The puppy's fur is covered in blood from a wound which I know has been caused by the person whose house it is. Even cruelly hurt, he wags his tail at me. I wake up in tears.

So, what are this series of dreams telling her?

Now is the moment to equip yourself with a notebook and pen. Take some time and examine the examples. List objects, colors, numbers or whatever in the dreams seems prominent to your eye. Try to pick out the key symbols and see if you can decipher their meanings. Can you place the category the dreams belong in? (More on categories soon, your best guess will do for now).

Pay attention to any dialogue and look carefully at the emotional response of the dreamer.

It's really important not to skip this step as focusing will help you to understand your own dreams more easily, as well as helping you to observe the hidden patterns within them.

So how did you do? Did you manage to make any sense out of the symbols? If not, don't worry. As with all things, practice makes – if not perfect, then at least much more proficient. Also, it is often more difficult to decipher someone else's dreams.

Okay! Let's crack open the symbols and meanings in those three dreams. We'll begin with the simplest – always a good place to start, I find.

The simplest dream to interpret is the middle one. As already stated, cars represent ourselves. In this case, my friend and her husband are traveling the same road but in separate cars indicating their, by then, separate lives. The placing is also significant: she's following him. Which describes their marriage perfectly. It was always obvious in the 30 years they spent together that his needs, hopes, wishes and dreams had precedence over hers. He takes the lower road, the left fork, indicating his breaking away from the original road they were on (their marriage). It also, then, represents the past, as he would no longer be in my friend's future. For me, the left-hand path, dependent on the rest of the dream content, has connotations of negativity or can be indicative of bad or even evil. In this case, the fact it was also the lower road signifies her husband's lack of conscience.

In this dream, the house, (my friend) serves a double meaning. Another woman is in her house (in her place as her husband's life partner). While she was trying to find her way, the overriding feeling was one of anxiety and tiredness.

The first dream is a little more complicated, but essentially it contains much of the same information. The car (her) is being driven by her husband (he is in control of her). The significance of the weather lies in pointing to the emotional context of the relationship (dark, heavy raindrops/tears, storm coming). His ignoring her pleas reflects his indifference to her wants and needs. She takes drastic action (throwing herself out of a moving car) and he, carrying on recklessly, dies, or, more correctly, she takes away his control and makes a stand against his actions and his feelings for her die. In reality, he presented her with a list of what he would expect from her if he stayed with her, and, for the first time, she took a stand and presented him with her own list.

The dust sheets signal the covering over of what was – this refers not just to their relationship but also to those things which had brought them to this point. That the dust sheets are located in a department store signifies the end of any financial support.

For me, the roof is not the mind – the upper floor of a building signifies the mind to me. The roof is that place of connection to spirit – in this situation you can perhaps read this as the life force, that which gives us our energy and will to go on living, and to which she clung to get her through – and the terror she had whilst he hunted her spoke of his ruthlessness in getting what he wanted. Even if that should prove seriously injurious to her. (She was at this time facing major surgery and could really have done with his support).

She survives, as shown by reaching her car and being in the driving seat. His apparition in the passenger seat signals the far-reaching consequences of his actions. So, even though he has relinquished control (no longer driving) he has left a lasting (undead or perhaps even eternal) impact on her life.

The last dream deals primarily with the fall out. The world as she knew it had ended in all practical ways. Dogs are commonly associated with loyalty but in this case the puppy signified her fear, vulnerability and lack of any means to oppose him, also the injury done to her. She had failed to take note of the previous dreams and now it was too late. It also encapsulated the fact that her whole life was tied up in her 30-year marriage, and, like the wounded puppy, even though there had been much in those years which left her wounded, she had clung to that life because she had nowhere else to go.

As I'm sure you've all probably pretty much guessed by now, these are in the category of predictive dreams and, a couple of months after the last one, her husband left for what he obviously considered to be greener pastures and she found herself without the much-needed post-surgery support she might have had a right to expect.

Although all three dreams essentially concern the same event, if you examine them closely you will see that there are significant differences.

In the first dream, she is essentially being warned that her husband has no care for her or her future. Not only are any feelings he may have once had, dead, he is also ruthless in going about getting what he wants. The dream warns her that the consequences of this will be far reaching. This proved true as one action of his in particular had devastating consequences for her, both emotionally and financially, which she is still living with.

The second dream tells her there is another woman involved and that things are coming to a head.

The last dream highlights the impact his leaving will have on her.

I would also like to touch on the power of three here. You will note there are *three* dreams, heralding an enormous tidal force of change and destruction heading her way. She's grateful now for her divorce but at the time it did devastate her world. Due largely to my prompting and the interest I was developing, she had been recording some of her own, more vivid, dreams for a couple of years, but at this point, she had no real understanding of the import of them. It was a hard lesson, but one thoroughly learned; she now never underestimates the value of her dreams.

When starting out on dream work, it is often only when you look back that you see with crystal clarity what your dream was telling you.

The dreams highlighted above are personal but here is an example of a predictive dream which did not focus on the dreamer.

On the 22nd of November 2021 a friend messaged to say: 'How strange, I had a dream this morning about a car ploughing into loads of people. It was very frightening.

Later, someone looked at the news and informed her of what had happened in Wisconsin, America, during a Christmas parade; five people killed. The power of our dreams!

Chapter 6

The Building Blocks

There are many everyday objects which your dreams may employ to pass on information to you. The trick being to determine what significance they hold for you. They will always have some. Even an object as ordinary as a toothbrush will have some association for the dreamer: Do they perhaps have bad memories of brushing their teeth? Or memories of someone they disliked forcing them to do so? Have they had problems with their teeth or are they proud of them?

Let us, for the moment, assume that the dreamer is someone proud of their teeth and slightly obsessive about cleaning them. Here, then, the emphasis could be on a few things. The association could be with a duty performed willingly and with pride. Or it could be a routine which makes the dreamer feel safe and grounded and in control: all is normal in my world.

But once you have recognized the association, what is the next step? How to progress from that to the meaning of the dream itself? The next thing to do is to look for clues in how the dream felt. Was there a feel-good factor or was there a sense of strain or discomfort in any way? Let's say, in this case, there was no discernable feeling either way. The next question then must be: what was happening in the dream? Perhaps there was nothing happening, just the toothbrush presenting itself to the dreamer? If so, this would likely be some kind of reminder. Maybe it's time for that checkup, or maybe the dreamer's oral hygiene has slipped recently?

Suppose, though, that in the dream the dreamer is brushing their teeth? This would show some kind of cleansing was needed. Perhaps the dreamer needs to clean up what they are saying about someone and stop spreading gossip or bad-mouthing someone.

Analyzing dreams is like doing a jig-saw puzzle, you have to find the pieces that fit together in order to build up the picture. Sometimes this is easy and sometimes it is quite difficult, and you will need patience and perseverance and often it is the short, simple dream, like the one above, which is actually the hardest to work out. But the rewards for your perseverance can be huge.

Let's take another example: a dream of eating bread. Again, the first step to analyzing this would be to ask yourself how you feel about bread. So, if bread is your least favorite thing in the universe, right up there alongside breaking a leg, chances are the dream signifies that you will have something negative to chew on shortly. Conversely, if you love it, something that will nourish your body or mind or spirit, or possibly all three, is on its way. But how about if you are someone who is totally neutral about bread? You can take it or leave it. Now is the time to start the detective work, piecing the puzzle together. Does bread hold any specific, perhaps religious, significance for you? What else was happening in the dream? How did you feel at the time? Were there any colors or dialogue? Did the bread give off an aroma? If so, did it smell good or the opposite? Did you get to taste it – delicious or total yuck? Is 'bread' a term you would think of in conjunction with money?

Okay, so you've explored all of the above and you still have no clue. At this point, if you own a standard dream interpretation book of symbols it might be time to take a peek. Does the explanation sit with you? If not, at least if nothing else, you now know your meaning doesn't lie along that particular trail. But just sometimes, particularly when beginning to work with dreams, the interpretation will resonate because your guiding self is using this as the only way to get through to you.

Sometimes, having carried out every investigation open to you, (including the methods I describe later in this chapter) the meaning of a dream will continue to be elusive. In this case, you can try talking the dream over with someone else to see if a fresh perspective can help, or, you may simply have to wait for another dream to cast further light on what is being communicated. If the dream information is significant, there will be another. You can also ask, prior to sleep, for further clarification. It is important to take stock of things that happen around the time of any dreams you find difficult to interpret, and this is where a dream diary can be of huge benefit.

Okay! Some more dreams for you to have a go at interpreting. Take time to consider each element of the dream, as well as the dream as a whole.

Dream One

I was walking in a beautiful garden. It was just lovely: lush and green and verdant, with waterfalls and streams and rivers. I was walking with a man I used to know and still keep in occasional touch with. His surname is Vickers but, in the dream, I felt he was a religious person of some denomination. We came to a river with a bridge across it and I wanted to cross to the other side, but the bridge wasn't accessible, and I couldn't see how to get across. But it didn't really seem to matter. I was just fine where I was.

Dream Two

I was battling the devil. We were facing each other across a desert strip. He hurled fiery bursts at me, and I hurled some kind of energy back at him. I knew I couldn't win but I wasn't afraid. All I had to do was keep him from winning.

Dream Three

I dreamed my stepmother came and asked me to forgive her. But I was still too hurt and angry, and I turned my back on her.

Dream Four

I dreamed my friend, who was dying of cancer came to me. She said, 'We've been trying to ring you, but we couldn't get hold of you, so I came to see you myself.'

Broadly speaking, dreams fall into a few categories. There is what I call the **clearing out** dream, the **predictive** dream and the **lucid** dream.

Dream One in the previous section falls into none of these. Instead, it is a rare type of dream: rare because such individuals are rare in today's busy, often challenging, world. This dream is an example of direct communication from the soul or higher self. It predicts nothing; it doesn't warn and there is nothing in the beauty of the scene which would indicate a need for any cleansing. The dreamer's companion's surname, Vickers (vicar) as well as the feeling of the dreamer as to their companion's occupation, immediately alerts us to a higher or spiritual connection and the beautiful garden is the dreamer's inner Garden of Eden. The easy acceptance of being unable to cross the bridge and the contentment with the present place of residence underlines the dreamer's contentment with life, as well as their awareness that death is not the end of consciousness (the bridge to the other side). A beautiful dream in every way.

Dream Two, although much less beautiful, is also an example of direct soul communication. This dreamer is being told that light and dark; good and evil exist in us all and, yes, even in the dreamer. And while we can never completely destroy the potential for evil within ourselves, we don't have to. All we need to do is to keep it in check; keep it from winning and overcoming the good within us.

On this note, I love the Cherokee Indian story of the two wolves.

Apologies to those, I suspect many, who will already be familiar with the story, but I do feel it's worth including for those who aren't.

'There is a terrible fight going on inside me,' a grandfather tells his young grandson. 'It is between two wolves. One is evil; filled with anger, envy, sorrow, regret, greed, arrogance, self-pity, guilt, resentment, inferiority, lies, false pride, superiority, and ego,' he continues. 'The other is good; he is filled with joy, peace, love, hope, serenity, humility, kindness, benevolence, empathy, generosity, truth, compassion, and faith.' Grandfather nods at his grandson. 'The same fight is going on inside you – and inside every other person too.'
The grandson thinks about it for a minute and then asks, 'Which wolf will win?'
The old Cherokee simply replies, 'The one you feed.'

On a more cosmic scale, the dream is also telling the dreamer to battle evil wherever they see it in the world.

Dreams Three and Four are another type of direct communication. These dreams are examples of one soul communicating with another. In the third dream, the dreamer's stepmother had recently died, having treated her stepson rather badly in the last year or so of her life.

The fourth dream couldn't be clearer, considering the life circumstances of the dreamer at the time, and sadly, as soon as she accessed her phone, she saw several missed phone calls and a voice mail asking her to ring her friend's daughter, who informed her that her mother, the dreamer's close friend, had passed in the night.

This is probably a good point at which to mention the phenomenon of shared dreams.

It can sometimes be that the same dream will be experienced

by more than one person. This can happen when the dream holds important information for members of a family perhaps, or friends or even work colleagues. Collective dreaming also occurs when something of wide import is about to take place, such as the devastation of the Twin Towers of the World Trade Centre when numerous, completely unconnected individuals shared the same warning, and sadly, prophetic dream. This is due to different individuals tapping into the same information from the ether, what Jung called the collective unconscious and what Cayce referred to as the Akashic Records. This second type of shared dreaming phenomenon also appears in a positive form mainly to creatives: inventors, writers, composers, poets, and such like. It is also possible for two individuals who are very close to regularly share their dreams, particularly if they share the same bed.

Although not truly a category at all, we will probably all experience the following type of dream several times:

The What the Heck Dream

Occasionally, you may have what you feel to be a powerful dream containing a very important communication but either you wake up before it's finished, or you can't remember the outcome or key message. In which case, you can try inducing an altered state of awareness in order to reconnect with the central message of the dream. Try to do this as soon as possible; that same morning if you can.

Sit down, close your eyes and center yourself. If you already practice meditation this will be relatively easy to achieve. For those who don't, the easiest and most effective way is to close your eyes and relax your body, starting with focusing on the feet and relaxing them, moving upward through the whole body, the legs, the lower back, the back, the shoulders, the arms, the neck, and into the head. Once that is accomplished, you should focus on your breath.

When ready, state your intention. I always do this three times, something like: I'm going back into last night's dream about (whatever the dream was about) to retrieve the information I need for the dream to fulfil its purpose in helping to guide and aid me.

In your mind, rerun the dream up to the last thing you can remember of it, and then just let it continue without any striving or influence from you.

You can also try the Gestalt method to aid recall. Placing two chairs (or pillows) across from each other, sit in one to ask relevant questions before moving to the other in order to provide answers. The key here is not to over-think and go with the first thing that comes into your head. So, it might go a bit like this:

Why can't I remember what came after I walked up the hill in my dream?
Because you don't want to remember.
Why?
You don't like what came next.
Is it important for me to remember?
Yes.
Did the woman hurt or upset me, or let me down in some way?
Yes.
If I could recall it, could I stop it happening?
No. But you would be better prepared to deal with it.

This conversation could continue in several directions, and until you had extracted sufficient information.

You can also take the part of each symbol or character you can remember from your dream. Here is one example. Perhaps you dreamed of a baby, snow, and a dog. You might, then, take the part of the dog saying: 'I am the dog and I represent – (it could be that, to you, the dog represents loyalty or happiness).

Then you would say: 'I am the baby and I represent –. Once you clearly know the meaning of your characters and symbols, you can allow them to talk with each other.

Generally speaking, dreams come in answer to questions, both asked and unasked, (those you don't yet know you'll need answers to or help with). But if you have a specific problem that you want assistance with, you can try 'calling' a dream to you. Just before sleep, you might simply ask; dream, please give me an insight into how I can improve my relationship with my sister. Or, dream, show me how I can heal the quarrel with my friend (insert name). Repeat the 'calling' three times.

You can also use this method to aid in healing. If you are ailing in some way then, before sleep, you can simply tell yourself you are well and healed. Or you can ask for guidance if you feel that you are in need of something, suggesting that tonight you will dream of whatever you are missing in your diet. You can use this method for anything you need answers to and tailor your 'calling' to your specific situation.

Ways to Enrich your Sleep and Dream Work
Stones and Crystals

Crystals are magnifiers and transmitters and have been used in practically all cultures and throughout history. The Celts referred to crystals as stones of power and the Egyptians used them to facilitate access to the inner realms. American Indians used crystals to aid in vision quests and in healing. Of course, shamans across the globe augment their powers with crystals and the lore of Atlantis is inextricably linked to the power and use of semi-precious stones.

There are several of these beautiful stones which can be helpful to those wanting to work with their dreams, but as always, go with your heart. If a beginner to either dreamwork or crystals, you may need to try out several to find those that most resonate with you.

Once you have made your choice, it is time to dedicate your crystal. Only program your stone for one thing at a time. Hold it to your third eye and speak your dedication. There are plenty of people who will tell you that you don't have to speak your dedication out loud and while I don't disagree with this, personally, I find that there is a power in the voice when dedications are said aloud that adds to the work being done. This dedication doesn't need to be a complicated thing. A simple 'I dedicate you dream crystal to aiding my dreaming so that I will remember and understand more of the message each dream brings for me' is just fine. If you wish, you can tailor this to be more specific. So, 'I dedicate you dream crystal to aiding my dreams to show me how to deepen my connection with spirit. Or 'I dedicate you dream crystal to aiding me with dreams which will provide me with insights into my future'.

If your focus for what information you need from your dreams changes, then simply cleanse your stone and re-dedicate it. Otherwise, you will only need to dedicate it once. Although you will need to cleanse and re-charge it regularly.

There are many ways to cleanse and recharge crystals. To cleanse your crystal, you can hold it under running water for three minutes (check first that it isn't a stone which can be damaged by water) or, the way I use myself most often, because it's easy, leave it buried in rice overnight. I keep recharging simple also, I'm all for ease. Either leave your stone in sunlight for six hours or in moonlight overnight, or, if you have a mother stone, you can simply leave your crystal in close proximity and let the amethyst do its loving work.

Once your crystal is ready, hold it in your left hand (your receptive hand) or place it on your third eye chakra as you focus on your intention to dream for a few moments. Once you're done, place the crystal under your pillow, on the bedside table or under the bed.

Amethyst

Amethyst is a gorgeous, rich purple, broad-spectrum crystal, often known as 'the mother stone', because it can be used to recharge all other crystals. This superb stone has so many amazing benefits it's hard to find something it doesn't work for.

Amethyst opens up intuition, it enhances psychic abilities and connection with Source. If you want to achieve lucid dreaming and connect with your higher self, thus enabling recall and interpretation of your dreams, amethyst may be the stone for you. Although a gentle stone, amethyst does amplify energy and if you are new to working with crystals there is a slight chance it may disturb your sleep.

Celestite

This is a calming stone which will help you to access the akashic records and explore your spiritual path.

Dream Quartz

Dream Quartz, also known as lodalite, lodolite, shaman quartz, shamanic dream quartz, garden quartz, and sometimes even phantom quartz, is a relatively newly discovered crystal. It is quartz with green prehnite and epidote. It is usually green, but the color can vary dependent on what other minerals are in the mix.

This crystal enables the archetypal patterns to communicate with the dreamer and opens the door to the superconscious. It's an extremely powerful crystal and excellent for astral travel and lucid dreams

Hemimorphite

This lovely blue crystal aids communication with Source. It stimulates the pineal gland and third eye to enable dream-time messages and assists the dreamer in interpreting them.

Herkimer Diamond

Despite their name, these are actually a type of quartz and thankfully, they're relatively easy to get and won't leave you bankrupt. They are a great crystal for any sort of dream work and perfect for helping you to remember the messages communicated by your dreams.

Moonstone

The moonstone, with its milky-white shimmer, is a gentle crystal and a good one for beginners to crystal energy to work with. It is connected to the cycles of the moon and its energy changes in harmony with those cycles. This stone is a psychic protector and as the moon is strongly connected to dream cycles the moonstone connects us more deeply to our dreamscapes.

Selenite

This translucent crystal is named for Selene, the Greek goddess of the moon and has a symbiotic relationship with the moon. It is a powerful stone and helpful for those wishing to gain understanding of their personal truths. It also serves as a key to the past and the future and as a tool for strengthening intuition and telepathic powers and can be used to aid telepathic communication during dreamtime.

Always dedicate your crystals. It is important to recognize that it is your intention which activates the stones and without serious intent, the crystals are unlikely to add much value to remembering and deciphering your dreams.

Different crystals may work better for you at different times in your life. As your life path changes you may find a stone which worked particularly well for you is now less conducive, whereas a stone which earlier didn't really resonate, now resonates strongly.

You may, of course, use more than one stone to aid your

dream work. However, I would advise using each stone on its own for at least three weeks in order to be able to gage whether that particular stone resonates with you and how much benefit it brings.

Dream Pillows

There are some herbs which enhance sleep and dreaming and if you are so inclined, you can make your own dream pillow using one, or a combination, of these.

Lavender is commonly used to aid restful sleep and mugwort is known to stimulate the third eye. The third eye, is, of course, the entry way to the inner realms. Chamomile is another aid to sleeping better.

To make your pillow, always choose good quality herbs and, as far as possible, use organic materials such as cotton or silk, silk is the best choice as it is an excellent medium of bioelectrical energy. If not allergic, use wool for the filling as again, it will help to align you with the flow of the planetary energy. The pillow can be as big or as little as you like.

Before going to sleep, hold your pillow to your face and inhale its fragrance. Keep it close during the night. Use your dream pillow only when you are intending to tune into your dreams.

Chapter 7

Mythology and Dreams

Once the dreamer arrives at a stage where he or she has more or less grasped the meanings of the more mundane symbols, perhaps even becoming comfortable with the meanings around numbers, the symbolism is likely to take on a wider dimension. At this point, an acquaintance with mythology and cosmic symbology will serve the dreamer well.

Animal symbolism plays a large part in mythology. The Babylonians gave us the Zodiac. The Egyptian gods and goddesses were often represented with animal heads. Bast is portrayed with the head of a cat. Sekhmet, the goddess of war and destruction, known as the lady of life, and the lady of terror, is depicted with the head of a lioness. Anubis is shown with the head of a Jackal.

Ganesh, the Hindu god of good fortune has the head of an elephant and Hanuman is an ape-god. Interestingly, in Hinduism, the first place in the hierarchy of being is not ascribed to man; the elephant and lion stand higher. Greek mythology is full of animal symbolism; Zeus, the father of the gods, was a shapeshifter who approached girls whom he desired as a bull, a swan, or an eagle. In Germanic mythology, the cat is sacred to the goddess Freya and the boar, raven and horse are sacred to Wotan. In the present-day, shamanic workers identify with animal spirit guides. Even in Christianity animal symbolism features strongly. St. Luke has the emblem of the ox, St John has the eagle, and St. Mark has the lion and Ezekiel's vision of a fiery chariot contained creatures with not only human faces but the faces of a lion, an eagle and an ox.

As you can see, a study of mythology, if only cursory, may yield a great deal of information to aid you in interpreting your dreams. Alternately, Google is always there when needed!

The serpent is a creature steeped in mythology, as is the dragon. The snake, in particular, often comes to us in dreams.

Now, the snake has come in for a lot of bad press, starting with the Bible and the tempting of Eve, who, in turn, tempted Adam (isn't it just always the woman's fault?). In fact, so much negativity has been piled on the snake that, instantly, for many, its appearance is linked to evil.

For some, though, among them Carl Gustav Jung, the serpent symbolizes knowledge and therefore wisdom. If you reject the biblical version of the snake's role (after all, the serpent is guilty only of offering Eve knowledge, and therefore choice, rather than leading her onto an evil path) and subscribe instead to the belief that in ages past a superior race, (as referenced in many origin stories from many cultures) referred to by some as watchers, or Grigori, walked the earth amongst us, and that Semjaza, their leader, and the fallen angel who loved a mortal woman more than his own kind, stood against them to bring wisdom to humanity both prior to and during his sojourn as the feathered serpent or rainbow dragon, Quetzalcoatl, the Aztec god of wind, air, and learning, then you will associate the serpent and the flying serpent, or dragon, both, with wisdom. This is true for many students of the mysteries.

There are further positive connotations for this much maligned creature. The caduceus, which features two snakes, was the staff carried by Hermes Trismegistus, the god of Divine wisdom. And the Rod of Asclepius, with its single snake curled around it, is a symbol adopted by the medical profession and stands for the knowledge which must be acquired prior to practicing medicine.

The cosmic serpent, Ouroboros, forms a ring with its tail in its mouth, and is a symbol of the "All-in-All": the totality of existence, infinity, and the cyclic nature of the cosmos.

In Hindu mythology Lord Vishnu is said to sleep whilst floating on the cosmic waters on the serpent Shesha. In the

Puranas, Shesha holds all the planets of the universe on his hoods and constantly sings the glories of Vishnu from all his mouths.

Whether you view the snake as good or evil, it is, from its beginnings, associated with knowledge and wisdom, either in a mystical or medical capacity.

Over time, though, there is no denying that the snake has become associated with evil in the collective consciousness and is therefore not completely without sin. But (and it's a BIG but) discerning the meaning of what dreaming about this creature really symbolizes for you, personally, involves taking very careful stock of what else was going on in your dream.

Questions to ask yourself

What color was it? Red most likely signals danger: the dreamer is entering a dangerous situation of some kind. Black is immediately associated with evil whereas, in fact, black often symbolizes the need to absorb – black absorbs all other colors into it – which can pertain to information, facts or even feelings. Electric blue, for me, is associated with high-octane power, which can be positive or negative.

The next question is how did you feel in the dream? Were you afraid, relaxed, curious, ambivalent? Another question to ask yourself is: what was the snake doing? Was it (excuse the pun) keeping a low profile? In which case it could be someone intent on doing you some sort of mischief – the proverbial 'snake in the grass'. Or was it clearly visible, or perhaps curled around an object, bringing you insight into some matter, or indicating something you need to take note of.

I had this dream twice:

A huge, translucent serpent reared over me (translucent and in full view – nothing to hide). It seemed to be asking a question and, although no words were spoken, I seemed to acquiesce to what it proposed. The enormous snake descended on me, swallowing me in entirety.

To me, the serpent represents wisdom, but before acquiescing to the snake swallowing me (immersing me in knowledge), I would have done well to remember that the path of acquiring wisdom is not an easy one. We learn most of our important life lessons through adversity.

Here is another dream for you to decipher:

I was with R. We decided to look round the market. There were some stairs to an upper level, and I said, half-joking, 'Don't go up there!' I knew if we did, I'd spend ages and be tempted to buy stuff. But he ignored me, and I followed him up the steps and through a door. Inside, it was very New Age and exotic, filled with color, as well as colorful, eccentric, characters.

We began to walk through to the back of the room, passing many stalls offering brightly colored scarfs and other arts and crafts. The room was dissected by a path running straight down the middle and as I stopped to examine one of the scarfs, R walked on, crossing to the right side of the room.

On the left, I saw some pretty scarfs and I was drawn to a blue one. I was so tempted, but then I reminded myself I had lots of scarfs and reluctantly put it down. I wandered along the rows of stalls until I reached the spot where the path split left and right. I wanted to go right, where R was, to look at some interesting stalls, but no matter how hard I tried, my feet refused to carry me right, taking me instead down the left-hand side of the room while R remained on the right side. Finally, I gave up and went to the left.

There was a blond, slim lady there who's skin was very pale, in fact, absolutely white. Her style of dress was unusual. She seemed to offer me help and I found myself in a reclining chair, which was black. She sat astride me and breathed into me, and I breathed into her. Then she put her tongue in my mouth, and I did the same with her – there was nothing sexual or romantic in this – it all had the feel of a process which I trusted would help me in some way. I placed my hands on her bottom, her dress had ridden up and she wasn't wearing any underwear.

She produced a bottle and sprayed it on my face and arms. There was a name on the label, something like 'Shining something' I sprayed her with it, spraying too much on her face, making her momentarily uncomfortable. I apologized for being too heavy-handed. She gave me the bottle and told me to apply it – I think whenever I'd bathed, but I'm not sure I've remembered that bit correctly.

We went into another room and R came in. Other people were there, and they wanted him to help move something. He was reluctant but he agreed, and they went off together. I went outside to get my shoes, which I'd taken off at some point, though I didn't remember doing so. I found them on a shoe rack: they were sandals, a bit old looking and dusty. I glanced down and two, different, sturdier, red, second-hand shoes were on my hands. I examined them but I didn't really like them, and I became aware of the smell of sweaty feet. I put them down and went to sit on a stool to put on my own sandals.

Suddenly, I realized I probably owed the white lady some money, so I went back to the room. She said I owed her ten pounds. I'm not sure but I think I paid her – I got the money out of my purse, anyway.

I left the market, and I knew R had gone. I was suddenly anxious to get home and get on with the work we'd planned on doing. I realized my feet were bare and thought about going back for my shoes, but when I looked at my watch it was late (twenty-to-three or maybe quarter-to-three). I was so anxious to get home I convinced myself my shoes were in my bag and just carried on in my bare feet. I was in the next town and the journey home seemed to take ages – time stretching, as it sometimes does in dreams. Throughout the dream I had problems hearing what people were saying.

Time to get out that notebook and pen again. This one is, as you'll have realized, a rather long and complex dream with plenty to get your teeth into. Remember to: list objects, colors, numbers or whatever in the dream seems prominent to you. Try to pick out the key symbols and see if you can decipher their meanings. Pay attention to the dialogue and acquaint yourself with the emotional response of the dreamer. First things first – what category would you put this into?

It actually crosses back and forth between predictive and direct soul communication.

The first part takes us to an upper level: for me, and for the dreamer, the upper level symbolizes the mind. The fact that she couldn't turn right to where her companion had gone signifies the temporary nature of the relationship (a parting of ways). The upper level (the mind) tells us the dreamer already knew this but was reluctant to accept the fact – she keeps trying to go right. The fact that she has difficulty hearing what people are saying signals that there is something she doesn't want to hear. The left path she is forced to take puts the relationship in the past. The blue scarf that catches her eye focuses attention on her throat (communication/voice) and the heart (emotions). Why the heart? Because scarfs generally, although worn around the neck, touch the heart space with their dangling end material. The color blue had no particular significance for the dreamer in a personal sense, but, as a student of spiritual matters, it carried the association for her of service. This translates as the dream telling her it would serve her heart and her emotions well if she spoke out about her concerns. Her realization that she has many scarfs relates to the many times she's tried to talk things through with this man, so she decides not to 'buy the scarf', in other words, not to speak out.

Then the dream becomes direct soul communication and indeed, an initiation of some sort.

The black chair and the pale or 'white lady' pertain to the yin and yang energies which flow through all creation. Additionally, the 'White Lady' is, of course, The White Goddess or Muse of the creative arts (the dreamer is a creative). But the association here goes beyond the realms of imagination and into the realms of intuition. The label on the bottle, the contents of which is liberally applied to both the dreamer and the White Goddess, points to the necessity of nurturing the shining spirit within. The lack of underwear calls attention to the bottom or anus. But this is a goddess and so the interpretation is not personal but cosmic. If we look toward the universal for meaning, we find Uranus, and the work of David Pond astrologer, author, speaker, and international workshop leader on the outer planets. Who writes:

> The outer three planets (**Uranus**, Neptune, and Pluto) are transpersonal, beyond the realm of the ego. They are aspects of your spiritual nature and deal with the soul's awakening and the growth of consciousness.
>
> He goes on to say: Uranus awakens you to a level of reality that is beyond the rational realm.[6]

Intuition, the fabled sixth sense, is a type of intelligence beyond the thinking mind.

Uranus is the conduit to a collective level of intelligence (Jung's collective unconscious and Cayce's Akasha or superconscious) from which pool the creative individual can access not only those creative flashes which become poetry or novels or films, but which also allow the individual to access other spheres of existence.

The dream now crosses back to predictive. The dreamer's companion goes off to help someone else, leaving her alone. The red shoes speak not of danger in this particular instance but of anger, the dreamer's anger at her companion's behavior. They smell unpleasant, warning her of unpleasantness to come. None of this is what she wants, signaled by her putting down the shoes.

In fact, very shortly after she had this dream, the dreamer discovered R was seeing someone else. He was reluctant to reveal this at first but decided he had little to lose (the dreamer acknowledged that the relationship between them was at rock bottom at this point).

The dream leaves the dreamer in no doubt that this relationship is over, (*I left the market and I knew R had gone*) showing her this in several different ways. The relationship had been very off and on again over the period the dreamer had been with this man, so perhaps the emphasis was felt to be necessary. Indeed, despite the dream, the dreamer went back to this man again, and again, the relationship failed, at which point she finally let go and did so easily, feeling she had done all she could to make it work.

In the dream, the dreamer was unsure of the time, either twenty to three or quarter past three. Taking twenty as two, the first would add up to five – two + three and the second to nine 15 + 3 = 18, 1 + 8 = 9. But actually, either number will do as the number five represents immediate change, while nine represents a finish or the coming to an end of something. In this case, the ten pounds, or the number ten, which signifies completion, underscores the inevitability of what will come to pass. Equally, it promises strength. Ten also signifies a return to the number one, which number, cosmically, represents the universe in all its expressions of the creative force. Viewed from a personal perspective, it is telling the dreamer that the experience of this particular relationship is over, completed. But it also informs her that she has the strength to accept this without undue disturbance to the psyche and that she will forge ahead on her creative and spiritual paths. The meaning of the dream is further emphasized by the fact that her companion goes off and leaves her alone, and the dreamer's sudden anxiety. She is unprepared for this ending, (bare feet) and she toys with going back to get her shoes (going back to the relationship) but then she persuades herself that she has them (persuades herself the relationship can be salvaged) and hurries home to get on with the work which needs doing, as, in fact, she eventually did. Subconsciously, this dream heralded a dramatic change for the dreamer as it prepared her on an unconscious level for the eventual termination of the relationship, helping her to accept its inevitable demise. Although she did return to R for a while, on questioning, she revealed that, this time, her mental and emotional attitude had shifted and she had been able to take a step back, so to speak.

N.B. If the dreamer had other, personal, associations to any of the numbers mentioned in this dream, or indeed, to any of the other material presented, then, of course, that meaning would take precedence. But given the rest of the content, we can be pretty certain that the correct meaning has been discerned in this context.

As always, with all symbols, it's the dreamer's association with the mythological representation which is key. So, if you dream about Thor, the Norse god of thunder, the sky, and agriculture, and the defender of Asgard, realm of the gods, and Midgard, the human realm, who is primarily associated with protection, and you are a student of or interested in Norse mythology, then this god's attributes are where the dream meaning lies. Thor's great strength is his main feature, but on the negative side, he has a quick temper, resents others' rules, and prefers direct action over discussion or planning when it comes to solving any problem. He is without guile or the capacity to deceive and can't recognize these qualities in others, so, he's often tricked by magical spells or shape-shifting entities which cause things to appear other than they are. Therefore, a dream of Thor for someone conversant with Norse mythology may be a warning of a difficult situation on the horizon. Or it may symbolize that the dreamer needs to be more patient or that they need to take care not to be tricked into something.

If, on the other hand, you dream of Thor and your only association is with the golden-haired hunk who plays this character in the Marvel films, then your interpretation could run along the lines of discontent with your present partner or signify your wish to be in a romantic relationship. It could even be a predictive dream, literally signaling that the man of your dreams is on his way.

Here is another dream to try:

I was with others, escaping from a foreign land. There was a wall with a hole in it which was blocked up. The hole led into a dark, lower space that was filled with water. One had to go through the hole, drop down, hold one's breath under water and swim through, following the light to the exit.

I was the last one to break through because I wanted to take things with me. I had been through the water twice before, but this time, I was worried that the last person before me had turned off the light and sealed up the exit.

What category did you place this dream in? I would place it in the category of the clearing out dream, where the dreamer's unconscious is turning over and working with the content of the dreamscape.

This dreamer is in a place where not only does she not understand the what and the why, it's also anxiety making enough that she wants to escape. (In reality, the dreamer had an uncomfortable situation going on, as well as anxiety related to her health. She knows she isn't the only one who has ever visited this place, and there are others there right now who also want to escape because, basically, it's not a great state of mind to be in.

Everyone who is in control of their emotions (at least most of the time) has a wall. With some it's impassable but the dreamer has a hole in the wall, which, although it's blocked, allows her access to her emotions when she's ready to acknowledge them and work with them. Water is almost always linked with emotions and the lower space speaks to the unconscious. That it's dark reflects the feelings she is accessing at this time when she goes there.

For me, this dream relates to a rite of passage, which the dictionary defines as a significant event in a transitional period of someone's life, and which those on a spiritual path experience many times, significantly, at moments when their faith is tested.

She was the last one to break through because she wanted to take things with her. She elects to take some of her emotional baggage with her as she is not prepared to cut herself off from her life experiences and the feelings associated with them. She's astute enough to know you lose something of yourself if you do that. The fact that the dreamer had been through the water twice before, making this the third time, is significant, as in actuality, the dreamer had experienced two previous events which had taken her to this same, dark place, but this time she was wondering when, and almost, if, it would end. But what the dreamer is really focused on is not losing her faith (the light). I use that term in whichever context applies to the dreamer, rather than in the traditional sense.

Another couple of dreams for you to hone your skills on:

Dream One

I was going up a hill in my car. There was a female friend in the passenger seat. The car started to slip backwards. I gave it more gas and still it kept slipping back. I applied the handbrake and it still continued slipping. Finally, as I was panicking and thinking the only thing to do was turn around, it got traction.

I turned left into a street which was much more level terrain and in which I felt I could park safely without risking the car sliding again. At this point, I seemed to be on my own, the female passenger having disappeared. Then I was looking at a couple who I somehow knew had been offered accommodation across the street from where I'd left the car. It was a lovely, quiet setting with a beautiful view. They were really happy and excited, and I was for them.

Then I was in a restaurant. It was quite dark inside. I was with a long-haired cat who I had to call back to me as she was about to wander off. There was a waitress, and she seemed a bit taken aback by my having a cat with me. The cat was rainbow colored: golds and browns and reds, pinks and yellows. She was really very beautiful.

My Interpretation

This dream offers the dreamer, who is going through a difficult patch, some positivity, and a promise that things will improve. Going uphill is always more of an effort than travelling on level ground. Sometimes it can be really challenging to get to the top of even a relatively short, although steep, incline. As we see here, the dreamer is really struggling and no matter what he attempts, he just can't gain traction. In reality, at the point at which the dreamer had this dream, his life was challenging in all respects. His career was not going the way he hoped it would and he was quite disillusioned with his prospects. His relationships were equally fraught with difficulties. He had become despondent and had all but given up, even, at his darkest moments, contemplating suicide.

He turns left, onto more level ground. This signifies his past, when, although far from ideal, his life had been less difficult, and he had been largely okay with what was. The fact that things were not ideal is revealed by his focus on the happy couple and being uplifted by their happiness. In contrast, he is alone, his female passenger having gone AWOL.

The restaurant signifies the need to nurture and care for himself. But the place is dark inside, echoing the way he feels inside himself. Even the beautiful cat is in the process of leaving him. The fact it is a restaurant and not the kitchen at home is good news. It signifies that this 'dark' period can be temporary, in fact, the time spent in it is entirely up to him and he can choose to leave at any moment. But wait! Isn't it frankly weird to take your pet cat to a restaurant? The waitress certainly thinks so. But the cat comes to him when called and the rainbow colors captivate him completely. The dream is telling him that he must be active if he wants to make the best out of his life (he must take steps if he wants to change things – he has to call the cat). And it may be that he needs to step outside of his usual habits and perhaps surprise himself as well as others. And if he does, then there may be gold at the end of that there rainbow. At the very least there are many different experiences (different colors) ahead of him.

Dream Two

I dreamed I'd caught a large fish. It was lying on the bedroom floor of my childhood home. I tried to club it to death to put it out of its misery, but the task was so horrible I couldn't stand to carry on and stopped. I was hoping it was dead. I felt so upset I left it and went away.

Then A came and I showed it to him and as I looked, I saw it wasn't dead. It had moved its tail. As I watched, it exhaled a breath that looked as it would if you breathed out in severely cold weather, a visible plume. A said it must be suffering every agony. I agreed and asked him if he would kill it for me and end its misery and he told me he would. I told him there was another fish, also not dead and still suffering, in another room, and could he kill that one also?

A then went into the kitchen and started to do the washing up. I was desperate for him to end the fishes' suffering and I asked him again to kill them and put them out of their misery. Then his brother, B, who, in the dream, was still only little, around seven, came. I thought he had mince pies in a box and told him not to eat them as they were stale, but he said, 'It's jello.'

I'm going to spend a short while here and use this dream as an example to highlight how truly vital it is to take the time to investigate your own associations to any dream symbology thoroughly, as well as examining your life circumstances during the period the dream you are analyzing occurred.

My Interpretation

If this were my dream, which it isn't, this is how I would interpret it. I've always associated the fish with knowledge. But, as I was brought up a catholic, I also associate the fish, or the ichthys or ichthus, to give the symbol its correct name, with Jesus. Indeed, the ichthus is also known, in common parlance, as the Jesus fish. The fish is given symbolic significance in several of the gospels, where it is connected to miracles and mystical events. I also connect the fish symbol to the astrological age of Pisces and to the element of water. But which of these associations fits this particular dream?

Generally, dreams of fish are positive omens, however, the dreamscape here suggests something very different.

Given my associations, I would place this in the predictive dream category and would feel it was trying to show me something heading my way that would bring me much pain and which I would find very hard to accept but which would bring spiritual growth (the number seven, the age B is in the dream). Although the fish, meaning knowledge, are out of their element (water is associated for me with the emotions) they are still creatures which belong in the water and so still retain that connection with the emotions for me. The first fish shows me that the atmosphere is freezing (its breath is a visible plume) so its message is chilling. It is suffering terribly, so much so that I'm driven to put it out of its misery. So, the knowledge it has for me is something which once revealed will cause me intense emotional suffering. This is further underscored by my associating it with Jesus Christ, who suffered terribly. The dreamscape is the childhood home, which I would associate with a cold and distant mother figure and a dysfunctional upbringing and would therefore link whatever was coming to family.

There are two suffering fish, therefore two things which, to know them, will cause me pain. Given the extended time the fish lie in torment and the struggle entailed in putting them out of their misery, I would further deduce that whatever was on the way was not a momentary thing and that my suffering would continue for a serious amount of time.

A is the dreamer's child and B is his brother. This would signal to me, if it were my dream, that my children were somehow the cause of any suffering I was about to experience, highlighted by the fact that even though A agrees to stop the misery, in fact, he does nothing of the sort, going off instead to do the washing up. This further signals that the power to stop my suffering lies with A but he needs to clean up his act.

His brother, B, is unconcerned and only wants to have a good time. The jello is interesting as both the dreamer and I are British and wouldn't normally use that word for jelly. However, both of us have taken our children to America, where we spent happy, carefree, holidays. So this reference highlights B's focus on his own enjoyment.

How the Dreamer Interpreted the Same Dream

The dreamer is a very spiritual individual and his association with fish symbology, while echoing some of my own, was focused primarily on the spiritual aspect symbolized by the ichthus. For him, the ichthus stands for the duality embodied in Jesus and which is the burden of all mankind. Therefore, its significance for him was mostly centered on the reflection of the eternal struggle between the spiritual and earthly nature and the dangers of desire, and so his spiritual and physical alignment with the material world. Again, this is supported in the dream by the fact that B is seven years old, seven, as I've already pointed out, being associated with spiritual growth.

The dreamer was at a place in his life when things were changing. His sons were now young men and beginning to make their own place in the world. His wife had sadly passed some years earlier, and he had some decisions to make around his own future. For him, the struggle and misery which featured strongly in the dreamscape were reflected in the choices he was faced with. Part of him wanted to go off and explore Costa Rica, with a view to perhaps settling in a spiritual community there. Another part worried that if he took this path he would lose touch with his sons, whom he loved very much and was very close to, which is what had happened with his own father (hence the setting being that of his childhood home). This was a particular worry as the eldest was displaying some attitudes which were unhelpful and which the dreamer wanted him to clean up (do the washing up) and the youngest was largely focused on materiality and enjoyment. This was a disappointment to the dreamer as he had walked his talk and had hoped his sons would be more spiritually orientated.

He had also recently met someone, and the relationship was developing well. But his new partner was completely against the idea of upping sticks and going off to pastures unknown. Following his heart's desire would almost certainly put an end to that relationship. But if he stayed, the relationship might not work out anyway, turning chilly, like the atmosphere in the dreamscape, particularly if he were left feeling resentful because it had cost him his dream. And, he reasoned, his sons' lives would eventually connect with his less and less anyway, as they pursued careers and started their own families.

Two, paths, hence two fish, both involving a degree of struggle and misery which he could see as lasting at least for an appreciable time. For the dreamer, this dream was an example of how the brain can continue to grapple with problems even while you sleep.

As you can see, although the symbolic associations of the two dreamers are not a million miles apart, the interpretations, when the symbol associations are closely examined and when life circumstances are taken into account, are quite different. Whereas I would interpret this dream as a warning, for the actual dreamer this represents his mind churning over the problems already present in his world.

Chapter 8

Common but Flexible Symbols

As well as the small number of symbols I've previously pointed to as having fairly universal meanings, there are some other common symbols it would be remise of me not to acknowledge. The reason I'm listing them separately is that these are much more variable and more open to individual interpretation.

Running

A common dream is where the dreamer is trying to run but it's as if something is holding them back and it feels as if they're moving through treacle. Generally, this dream symbolizes an attempt to run from some kind of adversity. The attempt is rarely successful.

However, if you were a professional athlete, or even someone whose fitness regime included regular running, it could be interpreted in a number of ways. For an athlete it could be speaking of difficulty in reaching a goal. For a regular runner its meaning might point to obstacles arising that could prevent them from sticking to their regime.

Ordinarily, running is generally, as already stated, an attempt, or a warning, to run from trouble, or a prediction of running into it. Running from a person in a dream can be a prediction of someone coming into the dreamer's life who will be a negative influence. It can also be an example of the subconscious, rather than the superconscious, going over old fears which haven't been satisfactorily dealt with, this would be particularly true if the dreamer has past experience of a traumatic relationship or event.

Flying

Dreams about flying often relate to wishful thinking, having unrealistic goals or an inflated sense of self-importance. However, flying is also common during astral projection. Unless very young, a dreamer who is astral traveling will almost certainly know that this is what they're engaged in.

Falling

A dream of falling generally relates to unrealistic goals, and ambitions beyond the dreamer's capability to carry out. But it can also be a literal warning. Jung describes a man inextricably involved in shady affairs who developed a passion for mountain climbing. In a dream, he saw himself stepping of a summit into empty space. Despite Jung's warnings that the dream foreshadowed his death, the man continued his climbing. Six months later he plunged to his death in a climbing accident. According to the guide, he suddenly appeared to let go of the rope, as if jumping into the air. Jung had interpreted the dream as the man's unconscious search for a definite way out of his difficulties. The aforementioned highlights the need to reference all dream symbology, first and foremost, to what is going on in your life.

Recurring Dreams of the Past

If you have recurring dreams of a past situation (or perhaps more than one), you need to look at how that situation worked out. If the outcome was good, then the dream is telling you that you're on the right path now. If the situation ended badly then the message is that you're repeating past mistakes.

Dreaming of an Ex

Another, common, recurring theme is dreaming of an ex, and there are myriad ways to interpret this one. If the breakup is recent, your brain may simply be dealing with the fallout: Who was largely to blame? Could you have done something differently? Could it have been saved? This process of identifying what went wrong can benefit future relationships, particularly if you're resistant, at that moment, to accepting the truth in a conscious, awake state. Of course, there is also a possibility that you're not over them yet and the dreams offer you a way to revisit that way of life until you are ready to let go and move on.

If you dream about an ex at the start of a new relationship, you are probably making a comparison in an effort to see if this time things could work out. If the relationship was a bad one involving any kind of abuse, then there is an element of PTSD to any recurrent dreams and the dreamer may need some additional help in order to start to rebuild their life.

Other interpretations could be that you're counting the cost of that past relationship in terms of the sacrifices you made as you tried to hold onto it, or before you had the courage to leave. It could also be that you're afraid you'll get hurt again. Another interpretation would be that something else in your life is making you unhappy. Or you may be struggling with forgiveness, or you could simply be missing some aspects of that life.

The best advice here, as always, is to look hard at your current circumstances and emotions to throw light on the meaning.

Chapter 9

More Practice Dreams

Below are a few more dreams to sharpen your skills on. As always, look at objects, colors, numbers or whatever in the dreams seems prominent to you. Try to pick out the key symbols and see if you can decipher their meanings. Do your best to categorize the dreams. Pay attention to the dialogue and acquaint yourself with the emotional response of the dreamer. Doing this work thoroughly now will help you immensely when you start to analyze your own dreams.

Let's start with a short, simple one:

> I dreamed Death was pushing a pram.
> This one is so easy you don't need to do much work to figure it out. For me (it's my dream) Death signals the end of something, and babies have always meant new beginnings to me. So, something is over but something new is right on its heels.

The next one is also fairly straightforward:

> I was doing exercises in a class with my dad.
> This dreamer's father has passed over, but he is often around and still worries about and wants to take care of her. The dream is telling the dreamer she needs to get more exercise to stay in good health.

How about this one:

> I dreamed I organized a wedding for a couple with a genetic

disorder. They had a baby who was healthy and didn't share the disorder.

The dreamer here is a perfectionist who sets himself very high standards. The dream is telling him that things don't have to be perfect to turn out well.

Or this one:

I dreamed my mum and I were laughing and joking together. Though short, this dream is truly sweet. In life, the dreamer's relationship with her mother was poor as the mother had mental health problems and was sometimes quite cruel to the dreamer. This dream shows the dreamer's forgiveness, thus freeing them both.

Okay, hopefully, things are beginning to become clearer for you and you're now noting how each dream is interpreted according to the dreamer and their circumstances.

Now one which is just a little bit more involved:

I was trying to hang a couple of ornaments and I couldn't quite reach. I asked P to help but he said he was on his way to work and didn't have time. I persisted, saying the job would only take a couple of minutes, and he hung them for me.
Although the dream is a little more involved than the previous ones, the message is simple: Persistence pays!
The dreamer here is trying to forge a career in a competitive market and was, at this point, asking herself if success was out of reach and if she should give up.

Now this one:

I dreamed I stood before a white teepee. The flap was lifted by an elderly Native American Indian who gestured for me to join him and the rest of the people sat in a circle on the ground inside. I went to step inside, but I couldn't. My feet couldn't cross the entrance.

This is a really positive dream. The white teepee is, of course, symbolic of the White Brotherhood. The invitation is letting the dreamer know she is on the right path. Even so, she isn't ready yet to take the place that awaits her.

Here is another dream from the same dreamer:

I dreamed Jesus held out his arms and on them were ribbons, or perhaps it was ropes. They were creamy white, four in number. He was offering them to me.

Again, a hugely positive dream, the creamy white is not yet the pure white of salvation, but it is a work in progress. The number four in this case is pointing to the elements: earth, air, fire and water – so the balance upon the earth, and the ability to rise above life's difficulties by looking within and working to harmonize the body, mind and spirit.

Geometrically, and for this particular dreamer, the number four is also represented by the cube and is symbolic of the body and the earth element: matter, stability, solidity, as well as eternal and unchanging truth, again pointing to balance achieved on the material plane. Here it also signifies the four lower chakras, or lower self, to the extent that integration is being achieved.

Okay, here are a few you may need to work at a bit more in order to analyze them. Time to get busy with your notebook and pen again.

1. I dreamed D and I got on the wrong bus. I wanted to hurry and catch the one going the other way, but he

wouldn't hurry. We ended up missing the bus and I started walking, but he hung back. I was really irritated at him. After a while I noticed it was now dusk and I realized I was being followed. I didn't turn around, but I knew it was D. He didn't try to catch up, just followed.

2. The following night the same dreamer had this dream: I was meeting with a philosophically minded discussion group. D was being an ass. I asked him to go home, and he did. When the meeting was finished, I drove to his house. I could see when he opened the door that he was in a difficult mood.
He said he wanted to show me something he'd got for me. He was out of it. He got a spider, a tarantula, and Mishka (a cat) was chasing it. I was scared it would bite her or me, but I didn't want to harm it. It kept coming for me. Eventually, I tired it out and put it on its back on my dinner plate. D had piled a heap of prawns on the plate, and I was eating them. Somehow the spider became covered by the prawns and when D moved the prawns off it, I could see maggots. The sight made me feel sick and I couldn't eat any more. D said he was in some sort of difficulty, which I felt was emotional and mental.

3. I was being asked to step into water – it was a pool of some kind. There was a man beside me who was also being asked to do the same. He was scared. But I could see through the water, and I could see that below me was a wide step, or some kind of platform, for me to stand on. Below the man there was just a thin rim like in a swimming pool. I stepped in with confidence and unafraid.

4. I dreamed I'd gone somewhere and met a guy. I felt he

didn't like me. Then I went to stay with a friend. I was looking for a new house and I found a fabulous one – loads of space, big rooms, full of light, loads of character – all on one floor.

I went outside and looking up, I saw that above the ground floor, it went up as a really high tower. I really loved the house, but I didn't want it to be where it was. I went back to my friend's and her husband got into bed with me and made advances. He told her I was beautiful. She didn't seem to mind what was going on, but I did. She apologized and I left. As I walked out, I saw the man I'd been attracted to but didn't think liked me. He asked me out for that evening. I remember feeling so happy I'd finally met someone I found attractive and who seemed a decent, regular, guy.

1. This is a predictive dream. At this point the dreamer is in a relationship which has some pretty major issues. Getting on the wrong bus signals just that – the relationship is heading in the wrong direction. The dreamer would like to work things out – go in the right direction. However, her partner is not willing to do anything to facilitate change. The dreamer sees herself becoming irritated enough that she walks away, but, although he is unwilling to put in the work to secure the relationship, he is unwilling to let go. He keeps following her.

In reality, the dreamer did in fact walk away and if the part of the dream in which D keeps following her seems a little stalkerish to you, well, in fact, this man's behavior after the breakup did constitute stalking. The dreamer had one, last, illuminating dream about this man after they parted where she dreamed she awoke, unable to move, due to sleep paralysis, and D was standing by the bed, looking down at her. Wondering how he could have got through a locked door, she fell back into a deep sleep.

2. The second dream uncovers, literally, the hidden aspects of D while also highlighting the difficulties this relationship presents. Basically, it is an example of the unconscious turning over and working through those aspects of both D and the relationship which the dreamer is tempted to ignore.

This man was often rude to the dreamer in public, as shown in the opening scene of the dream. And he was often very difficult to deal with in private, again shown in his mood when the dreamer drives to his home. He was also a substance abuser, revealed by being 'out of it'. The dreamer had suspected this, but the dream is firmly telling her it is so.

Spiders are commonly associated with traps or entanglement because of the webs they build to trap other insects.

Here I need to take a little aside to point out something important: For me, spiders are good creatures. They keep down the fly and insect population and I also associate them with Ariadne and Arachne, so there are spiritual and mystical connotations for me. However, and why I'm diversifying, the circumstances of this dream mean that the interpretation here, no matter what the dreamer's personal associations for spiders might be, must be negative. This man is striving to trap or entangle the dreamer, and yes, this is, to a point, normal courting behavior (we all strive to show ourselves in the best light possible to attract a potential mate). But this man is a deeply troubled individual and has many negative personality traits he is striving to keep hidden. This negative aspect is further exemplified by the fact the spider is a poisonous one. The dreamer has a growing awareness that all is not well, but she has patience, and she doesn't want to harm this man (she tires the spider out) and indeed, during the course of their time together, D did respond positively to her loving patience, as represented by the spider on its back, a vulnerable and exposed posture. However, the improvement was pretty much all to his benefit, while his negative traits, which caused the dreamer much unhappiness, stayed put.

The dreamer feels that the relationship can be nurturing, signified by her placing the creature on her plate, and D does also want it to be as he piles wholesome food on the plate, obscuring the poisonous nature of the tarantula. But the apparent goodness is rotten at its core, revealed by the maggots, re-enforcing the dreamer's growing realization of the extent of his emotional and mental difficulties.

3. This dream doesn't fit neatly into the basic categories. It is a type of direct communication, but this time, rather than coming from the higher self, it is the unconscious communicating with the dreamer.

Here, as it is mostly, the water is symbolic of emotions, and the dreamer being able to see through it to safety is being told that she shouldn't be afraid to trust her gut instincts and that she can work through whatever emotions she experiences without drowning in them.

4. This is a communication dream, although whether from the dreamer's unconscious or from the superconscious, I would hesitate to say. This dreamer has low self-esteem, as evidenced by the fact she meets someone she is attracted to and immediately decides he doesn't like her.

She goes to a friend, as we generally do when we need advice, but she is also working, perhaps unconsciously, on raising her self-esteem. (She is looking for a new house. Houses represent the dreamer.) And she finds one, a fabulous one. (This could be a communication from the superconscious.) But it isn't until she goes outside (steps outside of her negative mindset) that she realizes above the ground floor, the only floor she could initially see, there is more – a high tower – in which she is in danger of imprisoning herself (high towers represent isolation— remember Rapunzel? imprisoned and isolated in a tower) due to her insecurity.

She goes back to her friend, and to underscore her erroneous thinking, her friend's husband makes it plain he finds her attractive and her friend is fine with this (supportive of the idea that the dreamer is attractive). The dreamer, though, isn't and her friend apologizes. (It's going to take work for this woman to accept her worth.) As a final message, just to make sure she gets the point, the dream brings back the man she was attracted to on initial meeting, but who she had immediately decided didn't like her, and shows her how wrong she was.

.

Chapter 10

The Power of the Archetypes

I don't want to spend too much time on the archetypes; there is a mass of information out there for anyone who wants to study these in depth. But there is no denying their importance and a basic working knowledge is useful for anyone who wants to interpret their dreams.

C. G. Jung, who is credited with identifying the archetypes and who spent more than half a century exploring dreams and their symbols had this to say:

> I have come to the conclusion that dreams and their symbols are not stupid and meaningless. On the contrary, dreams provide the most interesting information for those who take the trouble to understand their symbols. The results, it is true, have little to do with such worldly concerns as buying and selling. But the meaning of life is not exhaustively explained by one's business life, nor is the deep desire of the human heart answered by a bank account.[7]

Jung believed that a symbol can only be classed as an archetype if it is at the same time both an image and an emotion. He stressed that a true archetype could not be consciously created as it was already in the subconscious, connecting to the life-force moving within the individual, and responded to the need of the moment when a new perspective was required. He noted that archetypes appeared in the dreams of those who were in situations that were life-threatening or life-transforming.

Some confusion has arisen around this subject, which is partly due to the different names attributed to any particular figure. There are, however, four figures whose identification remains consistent and on which Jung placed particular importance: The

Anima/Animus, The Self, The Shadow, and the Persona.

Here is a list of the archetypes which, in my experience, are most likely to make a guest appearance in dreams.

The Self

This is an archetype that represents the unified unconscious (what I call the superconscious or higher self) and the consciousness of a person. It is the inventor, the organizing center, and the source of dream images. Jung described it as the totality of the whole psyche, encompassing not only consciousness, and therefore the ego, but also the unconscious mind. The Self can be thought of as an inner guidance, different from the conscious personality, that can be connected with only through the investigation of one's own dreams. It may appear in dreams as a child or a circle, square, quaternity or mandala.

N.B. This is the archetype which is often present in those dreams which I refer to as being communication from the higher self and those I term as direct soul communication, although not those which are communication from one soul to another.

Mandalas

Jung used the Sanskrit word, mandala, meaning magic circle, to describe what the mandala is. These circular, most intricate, intrinsic, endlessly repeating and variable symbols are another representation of the Self, the wholeness of the personality, which, if all is well, is harmonious. The state of the mandala reveals the inner state of your own self. A tangled, maze-like or cobweb type of mandala points to confusion, a loss of your true self or danger.

The Persona

This is how we present ourselves to the world and represents all of the different social masks that we wear. In dreams this archetype can be represented by the dreamer themselves or by another figure.

The Shadow

This exists as part of the unconscious mind (as opposed to the superconscious) and is composed of repressed ideas, weaknesses, desires, instincts, and shortcomings.

This archetype represents all that is unacceptable not only to society, but also to our own personal morals and values. It's all those things we would like to deny ourselves being guilty of, such as envy, greed, prejudice, hate, and aggression. It also represents the darker side of the psyche: wildness, chaos, and the unknown.

N.B. *The devil may, but does not necessarily, represent the shadow.* In the dream mentioned previously in this book, it does, but the meaning would, as always, depend on the rest of the circumstances, both in the dream and in the life of the dreamer.

The Anima/Animus

According to Jung, the **Anima** is a feminine image in the male psyche, and the **Animus** is a male image in the female psyche. The anima/animus serves as the primary source of communication with the collective unconscious (what I term the superconscious).

Jung describes the animus as representing the masculine aspect in women while the anima represents the feminine aspect in men. The combined anima and animus are known as the syzygy or the divine couple. The syzygy represents completion, unification, and wholeness.

Amongst some spiritual and alternative belief systems the anima and animus are seen as the higher self or soul of the individual while in others, which take account of different planes, or levels of existence, it is thought that the individual, if male on the material plane, will be female on the next level, or body of existence, and male on the next, alternating right up to the highest level of being.

In dreams the anima and animus can be represented by figures of the opposite sex which impart some kind of knowledge or wisdom.

The Ruler or Father

This archetype is a strong, stable, figure who strives for excellence, and wants everyone to follow their lead. While well-motivated, the ruler/father can easily become a tyrant. This figure is likely to appear in the dreams of someone who feels they are in a situation where they lack control.

The Creator/Artist

Here is someone who loves to transform things. This archetype is clever, non-conformist, and self-sufficient, imaginative, and good-humored. It can also represent inconsistency and someone who spends more time thinking than actually doing. This archetype is often present in the dreams of entrepreneurs or artists, also daydreamers.

The Sage

This figure is a free thinker. Intellect and knowledge are their essence. This archetype's prime satisfaction comes from using their intelligence and analytical skills to understand the world and their being. This archetype often appears in the dreamscape of scientists and inventors.

The Jester

The Jester likes to laugh, even at themselves. With this archetype what you see is who they are, sans any masks. Their goal is to enjoy life. The negative side of the jester is that they can be lewd, lazy, and greedy. Comedians and those who stroll lightly through life encounter this archetype in their dreams.

The Mother or Caregiver

This archetype is all about offering maternal protection to those around them. The Mother/Caregiver wants to protect people from harm. Preventing any danger or risk from threatening other's wellbeing is what motivates their actions. Those in the caring professions often have dreams featuring this archetype.

The Innocent

This archetype sees the good in everyone and everything. The innocent also wants to please others and needs to feel as if they belong. People who are feeling vulnerable and those with low self-esteem may find this figure in their dreams.

The Hero

This archetype will fight for honor, refusing to give up even in the most dire circumstances. Determined and strong-willed individuals, particularly when motivated by injustice, may encounter this figure in their nighttime adventures.

The Orphan

This is an archetype who walks around with open wounds. It is symbolic of betrayal and disappointment. It radiates neediness. The Orphan often plays the victim but there is a calculated side to this archetype, as well as a manipulative streak. Those who find life in general to be a burden, or a struggle, may see this figure in their dreamscape.

The Wizard or Magician

According to Jung, this archetype is a symbol of regeneration and renewal, of constant growth and transformation. Those carving out a career for themselves or those seeking soul growth may be visited by this figure.

The Lover

This figure has a generous heart and is a sensitive individual. Feeling loved is as vital as air to this type. This archetype represents all that is pleasing to the senses and appreciates beauty in all forms. Everyone is open to receiving this archetype in their dreams.

As always, it is important to remember that it is the personal or, in Jung's words, 'numinous', meaning for the individual which will reveal the message that the archetype carries for you. If you are involved with someone, for example, and the Lover shows up in a dream, then, as always, you would need to look first at your relationship – are you truly smitten, in which case the Lover may be confirming that this is really it. Or do you have doubts or perhaps feel that your partner isn't providing what you need, in which case the Lover may be working to alert you to this fact.

Always consider what the numinous meaning of this figure is for you. Is the Lover an integral part of your being or an idea you distrust, or perhaps something else entirely?

The different factors would heavily influence the meaning carried by any archetype for the dreamer.

As well as observing and documenting the predictive power of dreams, Jung believed that the archetypes are not static patterns but dynamic factors which can work in the unconscious for long periods of time, skillfully arranging the life circumstances of an individual in order to bring about necessary life changing crisis. This idea is shared by many on a spiritual path, who will readily tell you that if you don't understand or heed the message life is sending you first time around, then life will hand you ever tougher experiences until you are finally unable to do anything other than change course.

There has been criticism of Jung's theory of archetypes as the psychic material is not presented systematically, but, as Jung claimed – and as many now agree – it is impossible to pin a universal meaning onto an archetype, as it must be interpreted in terms of the whole-life situation (a living experience charged with emotion) of the individual. This idea of interpreting in terms of the whole-life situation, of course, also applies to dreams themselves.

Chapter 11

Lucid Dreaming

The art and power of lucid dreaming deserves a book on its own, and indeed there are some good ones out there, but I'd be remiss if I failed to at least provide the reader with an overview of what some see as the most powerful of all types of dreams.

Like so much else, the power of dream walking in a conscious state has largely been lost to our modern cultures and brains. In the past, Aborigines put their 'dreamtime' to effective use and their advanced practitioners were highly regarded and consulted in times of need, and it is likely that some of the Christian saints were able to facilitate lucid dreaming. Nikola Tesla, one of the greatest minds of our time, was an avid lucid dreamer. He used his dream time to build and design his paradigm shifting invention, enabling him to perfect his technologies.

Nowadays, the shamans of South America and the Native American Indian tribes, as well as some Tibetan dream yoga practitioners, may still keep this skill alive in a pure form. However, generating lucid dreaming should not be confused with and is not the objective of the practice known as Tibetan dream yoga, which at its heart is a method by which to train the individual to experience pure non-duality, which is our original higher and natural state.

Interestingly, in the West, as people become more spiritually aware, there is a growing interest in lucid dreaming and its possibilities and there are those who would seem to have a natural ability in this area.

Conventional dream interpretation relies on the rational mind's ability to make sense of the symbols presented in our dreams, and make no mistake, understanding our dreams can be of significant benefit to the individual. Lucid dreaming, however, opens up the process exponentially by allowing the dreamer to directly talk to and interact with his or her dream figures.

Lucid dreaming is a state in which the dreamer knows they are dreaming. There are, however, different levels to that conscious awareness. For some lucid dreamers, their awareness in the dream state is pretty much equal to when they're awake and making conscious sense of their reality. For others, the lucid dreaming state is more tenuous in that they momentarily, without any type of prompt, realize they are dreaming but that realization slips quickly from their grasp. This same, momentary realization may also come about because the dreamer recognizes some kind of dream sign, such as an impossibility taking place within their dream. This could be something like talking to a deceased person or piloting a plane when they wouldn't have the first clue how to in waking life, or a train lifting into the air and floating over a mountain top.

In addition to these, in his excellent book *Going Within in a Time of Crisis*, P.T. Mistlberger provides a list of universal lucid dream signs:

1. Electronics fail: Electronics usually do not work or do not work correctly in dreams. No one knows why, but it could be because modern technology is so complicated the dreaming brain cannot duplicate it.

2. Incorrect lighting: Many times, the lighting for a situation will not be correct. It will either be too dark or too light. Another noticeable dream sign is that attempts to change the lighting do not work. Quick changes in light require recalculation of colors and shadows, which seems to be too much work for the dreaming brain. Shadows may also look distorted or go in the wrong direction.

3. Deformation: Animals, people, objects, and scenery often look strange in dreams. The object of attention tends to

be larger than everything in its surroundings. Noticing anything misshapen should be an obvious dream sign, however it tends to be the hardest one to pick up on.

4. Illegible Text: Reading and writing tends to be difficult or impossible in dreams. If text seems blurry or jumbled together, it should be a clear dream sign. Text may also constantly change and never appear to be the same message twice. This also works with digital clocks.[8]

It can be that the lucid dreamer holds onto the realization that they're dreaming but their awareness is vague, and they continue to let the dream unfold as it will, without any interaction, and it's really only when they awaken that their realization crystalizes.

Most lucid dreamers fall into the category of recognizing they are in a dream but that is where their consciousness starts and ends.

However, some dreamers go beyond the above stage and the dreamer, recognizing that they are in a dream, consciously tries to take charge of the dream scenario by making changes to the content.

When you start to remember your dreams, you may discover that they sometimes contain people who are strangers, usually referred to by lucid dreamers as 'the others', as in 'this other woman was there' 'this other man …' and so on.

There is much to be gained if the dreamer is able to communicate with these others. It is then possible to question them regarding the reasons for the dream scenario and its meaning and so make informed changes to the dream content which can be beneficial in your waking life.

There are several methods you can use to train yourself in the art of lucid dreaming. One of the easiest and, to my mind, best ways for a beginner, as popularized by Carlos Castaneda, is to set the intention of seeing our hands in our dreams. So, immediately prior to falling asleep, you suggest to yourself that tonight, you will see your hands in your dreams. Visualize holding the backs of your hands up to your face. You don't need to spend long on this, thirty or forty seconds is sufficient, a minute at the outside.

You can also focus on seeing your feet in your dreams using the same method. I find it easier to see my hands but it's whatever works best for you. With practice, both methods can serve as triggers to the awareness that we are, in fact, in a dream state.

Prior to achieving full success, dreamers will often have several dreams in which their hands or feet feature in a peripheral way. They may dream of opening a door or washing their hands or holding onto an item or, commonly, of driving a car. But it is only on awakening and reviewing the dream content that they become aware of the significance of what they have seen. Eventually, though, the dreamer will achieve a sort of clarity of focus on significant objects and realize they are dreaming while still in the dream.

At this point it is common to awake immediately you recognize that is what is happening. The best way to overcome this is to avoid that sharp focus on the hands or feet, or other significant object, for too long and instead divert the attention to other things in the dreamscape. Again, it may take a bit of perseverance but eventually, you will be able to escape being ejected from the dream.

Another, similar, technique is to suggest to yourself that you will recognize any impossibilities or 'dream signs' while dreaming. You can also try rubbing your hands together in the dream.

Here are some further ways to induce lucid dreams, these should be used in conjunction with the methods suggested above. One idea is that when you awake from a dream, you immediately try to recall what it was about. Once you have the details, you then mentally relive the dream, imagining that you are still dreaming but awake inside the dream while you replay it in your mind. This method is said to dramatically increase lucid dreams if persevered with. Ideally, you would then fall back to sleep again to increase your chances of having a lucid dream. However, I'm rarely able to do this and I've still found the method to be most effective, although it has taken serious perseverance for it to begin to show results.

Another technique is to attempt to hold onto consciousness as you fall asleep. Best reserved for early morning or afternoon nap times, this method usually only works in the REM stage of sleep, so only after you have already slept for several hours.

Other ways to anchor consciousness in order to carry it into the dreamscape can be by focusing on the breath or being strongly aware of the body.

The wake and go back to bed method is one I've never tried but if combined with setting an intention and visualization it is regarded as being highly successful. The idea is to set your alarm to go off after you have slept for five or six hours. You then get up and stay awake for an hour or so before returning to bed to set an intention and employ visualization as you fall back to sleep.

Here are a few other things you can try in order to prolong your dream state:

- Should you awake, continue doing whatever you were just doing in the dream and try to convince yourself you're still in the dream.
- Fall backward or spin around in the dream.

There is one last type of lucid dreaming – generally only available to those who practice dream yoga – which is to use the dream state as a steppingstone by allowing the dream content to fall away in order to concentrate the consciousness on higher states, such as communicating with advanced beings.

Dream yoga is a term coined in the West for the high-level dream work practiced by Tibetan Shamans and some schools of Tibetan Buddhism. Below is a technique to use to aid in this practice.

1. Before going to sleep, send out a few positive thoughts to others, wishing them well, etc.
2. Remind yourself that you will remember your dreams tonight. Tibetan tradition generally recommends that you lay on your side – women on their left side, men on their right side.
3. Repeat the following simple prayer:
   May I have a clear dream. May I have a lucid dream. May I understand myself through dreaming.
   Repeat this several times with sincerity (either out loud, or internally). Then visualize a symbol in your throat chakra. This symbol should be visualized in luminous red. You can use the English letter 'A'. Hold this visualization for as long as you can as you fall asleep.[9]

The practice of dream yoga, in particular via the process of falling asleep consciously, is a means by which to experience higher states of reality and non-duality.

Chapter 12

A Few Final Practice Dreams

Dream One: I dreamed I was in a cookery class, and we'd been asked to make some mince pies. We were asked to work with a partner. My partner seemed really nice. She was interested in what we were doing and chatty. But, when we started to work, I realized she didn't want to actually do anything, and I was left doing all the work on my own.

Dream Two: Dreamed I was driving my car. I came to a signpost and decided instead of going straight on, I would go via the M6 which was on the left. I was thinking, I need the M6 to go home. Immediately, I turned onto the M6 I was overcome with tiredness. I was so tired I couldn't open my eyes. I was driving with my eyes closed as lorries and other traffic passed me and surrounded me. I knew I should pull over and take a rest and sleep for a bit because what I was doing was so dangerous. But it was difficult to get over onto the inside and find a place to stop because I couldn't open my eyes.

Dream Three: I dreamed some man wanted to murder me and that I was to be married but I didn't want to be.

As ever, look closely at the detail; objects, colors, numbers or whatever in the dreams seems prominent to you. Try to pick out the key symbols and see if you can decipher their meanings. Do your best to categorize the dreams. Pay attention to the dialogue and acquaint yourself with the emotional response of the dreamer.

Let's start with the easiest; dream three. This is an anxiety dream and belongs in the clearing out category. This dreamer is in a difficult situation. She feels threatened and that she is being pressured into something she doesn't want. Marriage equals commitment to the dreamer.

The first dream in this chapter is also pretty clear. It is a warning that the dreamer is being taken advantage of by someone who, on the surface, seems very cooperative. Although not a neat fit, this does fall into the predictive category as the dreamer was not aware of the situation prior to having this dream. Only with hindsight was she able to see the truth – for this relationship to work, the dreamer would have to be the one who did all the nurturing work.

The middle dream is a little more complex. The left side in dreams usually represents the past. The fact that the motorway (a fast road), is on the left signals the dreamer's urgent need to get away from the present, where the situation is difficult and stressful. The number six, M6, has connotations of beauty – the beauty he had in his past and which he longs for in the face of his present inability to cope with his difficulties. Traffic passing him points toward his feeling of lack of progress and that other people seem to be ahead of him in achieving their dreams and goals. Traffic surrounding him represents the hustle and bustle of life which he currently feels surrounded and overwhelmed by.

When he attempts to go back to the past (takes the M6) he is immediately exhausted – the dream is telling him that going back to his past is beyond his power. The dreamer, though, closes his eyes as he does not want to acknowledge (see) this. In closing his eyes, he is driving blind and in not facing up to the fact that the past is gone and cannot be revived, he can't see where his future is taking him either. He needs to pull over and take a break – he needs to step back from life, literally take a break, regroup, and take a fresh look at his problems when he is in a better frame of mind to deal with them. Unfortunately, presently, he can't see a way to do this.

Conclusion

I set out to write this book hoping it would help people to understand what a valuable source of information and help dreams can be, and to enable them to understand the symbols and content of their own dreams, and therefore be able to harness that power. I sincerely hope I've succeeded in doing that.

I also very much hope that along the way I've managed to make this endeavor engaging, as well as informative. With a little patience anyone can become proficient in dream analysis and the rewards for that perseverance can be of great value and possibly life changing. I would suggest taking small steps at first so that you avoid overwhelm. If you struggle to remember your dreams, then start by recording what you do manage to recall of them, writing them down as soon as you awake. If you are already fairly good at recollecting them, then begin by keeping a dream diary. Read through what you've recorded at least once a week, in this way you will start to engage with your dreams more strongly and spark an interest in knowing what they actually mean.

Always remember:

- Take the time to consider each element of the dream as well as the dream as a whole.
- In the beginning, you may want to check the standard interpretations of your symbols to see if they resonate with you and I hope that you will find the lists of symbols in this book helpful. But always, always take the time to seriously study a symbol to discover its personal meaning to you. If you look online, you will find numerous different interpretations of dream symbology, which only goes to show that although many things have

similar associations, there are also some wide differences. Only the dreamer can truly know the meaning of a dream. So always consider the personal associations you have with any symbol and ask yourself if they hold more significance than the standard interpretations.

- Think about any dialogue and who was speaking.
- Keep in mind your emotional reaction to your dream.
- If you decide to make a serious study of dream interpretation, then one good way of furthering your studies is to either join or form your own dream study group.
- This is easier now than ever before due to the reach of social media. A word of caution, though, if you do form a group, you will need to spend some time building trust as opening yourself up through the medium of your dreams can leave you vulnerable.
- Once the group has become a unit, you will need to ensure that each person is given enough time to share their dream or dreams, if it is a series. It is important to listen carefully to what each person shares. Pay attention to the exact words they use to describe their dreamscape. Receiving new input in this way can be truly helpful, but again, it is crucial to remember to only take on board those things which resonate with you.

Once the interest is there, then the work necessary in order to understand your dreams becomes a labor of love, and, as with any labor of love, enjoyable rather than onerous.

After all:

Dreams are illustrations from the book your
soul is writing about you.
~ **Marsha Norman.** Author and Dramatist[10]

References

1. https://beingpoint.com/dreams-are-todays-answers-to-tom orrows-questions-edgarcayce/#:~:text=%E2%80%9CDream s%20Are%20Today's%20Answers%20To%20Tomorrow's% 20Questions%E2%80%9D%20%E2%80%93%20Edgar%20 Cayce

2. Holy Bible (Book of Genesis, 41: 1-57) New International Version, (1984)

3. *https://www.famousscientists.org/7-great-examples-of-scientific-discoveries-made-in-dreams/*

4. http://jungcurrents.com/carl-jung-ten-quotations-on-dreams

5. https://lonerwolf.com/meaning-of-numbers/

6. https://www.llewellyn.com/journal/article/2789

7. Jung, Carl, *Man and his Symbols*, Picador (1978) pg. 93

8. Mistlberger, P.T. *Resilience Going Within in a Time of Crisis*, Changemakers Books, (2020) pg. 63

9. Mistlberger, P.T. *Resilience Going Within in a Time of Crisis*, Changemakers Books, (2020) pg. 64

10. https://www.goodreads.com/quotes/45102-dreams-are-illustrations-from-the-book-your-soul-is-writing

Bibliography

Sechrist, Elsie, *Dreams – Your Magic Mirror*, Cowles Education
    Corporation (1968)

Jung, Carl, *Man and his Symbols*, Picador (1978)

Jung, Carl, *Memories, Dreams, Reflections*, Fontana Press (1995)

Denise Linn, *Pocketful of Dreams*, Triple Five Publishing (1988)

Sugrue, Thomas, *Story of Edgar Cayce – There is a River*, A.R.E.
    Press (1997)

https://www.brettlarkin.com/chakra-colors-what-do-chakra-
    colors-mean/

Acknowledgements

Grateful thanks, as always, go to Maria Moloney Wilbrink, for her help and advice. Cecilia Finnerty and Patricia Spence, whose support gets me through. Thank you also to Adam Bradbury for his thoughtful suggestions.

About the Author

Krystina Sypniewski worked for ten years as a hypnotherapist and has worked with dreams for the past twenty years. She has studied Astro-Shamanism at the Findhorn Foundation and Shamanism with Julie Wise. She spent several years as a member of The Inner Light and other Kabbalistic organizations as well as undertaking a course in Tarot reading and psychometry in Liverpool, where she worked as a healer. She has an MA in Creative Writing and is a published author. Currently she lives with her cat LL, who is doing a great job in educating her on the finer points of animal communication.

Other Books

Mistflower the Loneliest Mouse, Our Street Books.
ISBN 978-1-78099-468-0

MOON
BOOKS

PAGANISM & SHAMANISM

What is Paganism? A religion, a spirituality, an alternative belief system, nature worship? You can find support for all these definitions (and many more) in dictionaries, encyclopaedias, and text books of religion, but subscribe to any one and the truth will evade you. Above all Paganism is a creative pursuit, an encounter with reality, an exploration of meaning and an expression of the soul. Druids, Heathens, Wiccans and others, all contribute their insights and literary riches to the Pagan tradition. Moon Books invites you to begin or to deepen your own encounter, right here, right now.

If you have enjoyed this book, why not tell other readers by posting a review on your preferred book site.

Recent bestsellers from Moon Books are:

Journey to the Dark Goddess
How to Return to Your Soul
Jane Meredith
Discover the powerful secrets of the Dark Goddess and
transform your depression, grief and pain into healing
and integration.
Paperback: 978-1-84694-677-6 ebook: 978-1-78099-223-5

Shamanic Reiki
Expanded Ways of Working with Universal Life Force Energy
Llyn Roberts, Robert Levy
Shamanism and Reiki are each powerful ways of healing; together,
their power multiplies. *Shamanic Reiki* introduces techniques to
help healers and Reiki practitioners tap ancient healing wisdom.
Paperback: 978-1-84694-037-8 ebook: 978-1-84694-650-9

Pagan Portals – The Awen Alone
Walking the Path of the Solitary Druid
Joanna van der Hoeven
An introductory guide for the solitary Druid, *The Awen Alone* will
accompany you as you explore, and seek out your own place
within the natural world.
Paperback: 978-1-78279-547-6 ebook: 978-1-78279-546-9

A Kitchen Witch's World of Magical Herbs & Plants
Rachel Patterson
A journey into the magical world of herbs and plants, filled with
magical uses, folklore, history and practical magic. By popular
writer, blogger and kitchen witch, Tansy Firedragon.
Paperback: 978-1-78279-621-3 ebook: 978-1-78279-620-6

Medicine for the Soul
The Complete Book of Shamanic Healing
Ross Heaven
All you will ever need to know about shamanic healing and how to
become your own shaman...
Paperback: 978-1-78099-419-2 ebook: 978-1-78099-420-8

Shaman Pathways – The Druid Shaman
Exploring the Celtic Otherworld
Danu Forest
A practical guide to Celtic shamanism with exercises and
techniques as well as traditional lore for exploring the Celtic
Otherworld.
Paperback: 978-1-78099-615-8 ebook: 978-1-78099-616-5

Traditional Witchcraft for the Woods and Forests
A Witch's Guide to the Woodland with Guided Meditations and
Pathworking
Mélusine Draco
A Witch's guide to walking alone in the woods, with guided
meditations and pathworking.
Paperback: 978-1-84694-803-9 ebook: 978-1-84694-804-6

Wild Earth, Wild Soul
A Manual for an Ecstatic Culture
Bill Pfeiffer
Imagine a nature-based culture so alive and so connected,
spreading like wildfire. This book is the first flame...
Paperback: 978-1-78099-187-0 ebook: 978-1-78099-188-7

Naming the Goddess
Trevor Greenfield
Naming the Goddess is written by over eighty adherents and
scholars of Goddess and Goddess Spirituality.
Paperback: 978-1-78279-476-9 ebook: 978-1-78279-475-2

Shapeshifting into Higher Consciousness
Heal and Transform Yourself and Our World with Ancient
Shamanic and Modern Methods
Llyn Roberts
Ancient and modern methods that you can use every day to
transform yourself and make a positive difference in the world.
Paperback: 978-1-84694-843-5 ebook: 978-1-84694-844-2

Readers of ebooks can buy or view any of these bestsellers by
clicking on the live link in the title. Most titles are published in
paperback and as an ebook. Paperbacks are available in traditional
bookshops. Both print and ebook formats are available online.

Find more titles and sign up to our readers' newsletter at
http://www.johnhuntpublishing.com/paganism
Follow us on Facebook at https://www.facebook.com/MoonBooks
and Twitter at https://twitter.com/MoonBooksJHP